BREAKING

Narcissistic Abuse

A Complete Guide to Emotional Recovery by Recognizing and Identifying Narcissistic Abuse, Overcoming Toxic Relationships, and Reclaiming Your Life

CAMERON J. CLARK

Contents

PART 3: RECLAIM

Repel Narcissists by Developing a Healthy Sense of Self-Worth, Setting Boundaries, and Taking Control of Your Life Narrative

Introduction

*Nice people don't necessarily fall in
love with nice people.*

–JONATHAN FRANZEN

The Wolf in Sheep Clothing

Four years ago, Tanya believed she had found her missing puzzle piece—let's call him Mr. X—the man who would rescue her from nearly a decade-long life of singlehood. They had met online on a popular dating app and began chatting instantaneously.

Mr. X wasn't like the average guy you pass on the street. *Something about this particular gentleman was special*. It wasn't about his looks or how much money he had (at that time he was unemployed and living with his folks). What made him different was how charming, attentive, and intuitive he was to Tanya's needs.

The relationship progressed rapidly. Within a few days, they were exchanging heart emojis and speaking about their plans for the future. He sounded serious about finding a job to buy a property big enough for both of them and even suggesting an engagement.

Everything felt right at the time, so Tanya was happy to follow his lead. The couple continued to chat over the phone before meeting face-to-face. Tanya decided to plan the coffee date because she had insisted on meeting up with him (they only lived five miles apart after all). She told him it was her treat since he was unemployed and couldn't afford to take her out on an extravagant date.

On the coffee date, Mr. X was everything Tanya had envisioned. He dressed well, smelled of expensive cologne, and spoke with an Ivy League alumni accent. He did all the gentleman-like behaviors, like pulling out the chair for her, ordering the beverages, and making sure she was comfortable. Toward the end of the date, he expressed wanting to spend more time with her and suggested they should go back to her house. She agreed and the two of them enjoyed a romantic evening together.

The morning after, things started to take a strange turn for the worse. Tanya overheard Mr. X arguing over the phone with what seemed to be his parents with intense rage. He ended the call with the words, "I'm not coming back!" and threw the cell phone on the couch. A few minutes later, Tanya found him sobbing with tears. He looked beaten down and hopeless, a state that she couldn't bear to see him in. She opened her house to him and said that he could stay for as long as he needed. *In hindsight, this was the biggest mistake she could make.*

Tanya soon learned that Mr. X had frequent intense anger outbursts, which were triggered by the smallest inconveniences. For example, he would yell at her for coming home late from work, forgetting to buy grocery items on the shopping list, or speaking too loud on the phone with her girlfriends. Tanya also learned that Mr. X wasn't prepared to find a proper job because he felt that no company could afford him. Instead, he would come up with spontaneous business ideas and obsess over them for weeks before changing his mind and going back to the drawing board.

He was financially reliant on Tanya to provide shelter, food, and entertainment (every once in a while). He would suggest outings but expect her to cover the bill. Whenever she would attempt to draw boundaries, Mr. X would guilt-trip her and imply that she was stingy and didn't care about anyone but herself.

Two years went by, and Mr. X became more cold, aggressive, and distant. Even though they were a couple, they lived like roommates who tolerated each other. Tanya felt underappreciated for the efforts she was making to nurture the relationship. The worst part was she couldn't voice her concerns out of fear of Mr. X's violent rage and insensitive comments.

One Saturday morning, while lying in bed, Tanya had a lightbulb moment. She realized that she was in an abusive relationship and that what once felt like "love" between her and Mr. X was an unhealthy attachment. Looking over at him fast asleep in a fetal position, she said inside her head, "I want out!" Over the next month, she planned her exit strategy from the relationship and finally broke up with Mr. X.

Narcissism Is More Subtle Than You Think

There are many women (and men) who have similar horrific dating stories as Tanya, who have survived narcissistic relationships. A common observation made by them is that their narcissistic partner didn't seem like a monster at the beginning. The reality is that real narcissists don't come across as dangerous or manipulative when you first meet them. If they did, their deception wouldn't work. Instead, they must present themselves as the ideal bachelor or bachelorette who is trustworthy and irresistible.

In the dating world, narcissists are known as the "bad boys" or "Casanovas" who can capture your heart with a smile and a promise.

They have a way with words and a strong sixth sense to know what you are thinking and feeling. Of course, this facade is only kept during the initial or honeymoon phase, and after a while, their true colors are revealed.

Even though narcissism has been the subject of social media commentary and song lyrics for many decades, it is a real medical condition that affects 5% of the U.S. population (75% of them are men) (Cleveland Clinic, 2014). The formal name for the condition is narcissistic personality disorder (NPD), which is the excessive need to feel important that distorts reality and negatively impacts relationships. Not everyone with narcissistic traits will be diagnosed with NPD, which is why seeking a professional diagnosis is important.

The purpose of this book is to shed light on narcissism and explore the many ways it manifests and impacts the quality of romantic relationships. You will learn how to spot narcissists from a mile away and understand the psychology behind their manipulative behaviors. Moreover, the book will offer several options for seeking support and healing as well as techniques to reconnect with yourself, build a strong sense of self, and take back your power!

Practicing the 3 Rs

Identifying narcissists is only the first step. Once you are aware of who they truly are, you must have a plan on how you are going to engage with them moving forward. This is why the "3 Rs" are critical for breaking free from narcissistic abuse.

The book is divided into three parts to outline three main strategies of how to deal decisively with narcissists. You can refer to these three strategies as the "3 Rs" which stand for:

- **Recognize:** Understand patterns of narcissistic abuse and manipulation tactics used to psychologically break you down.
- **Respond**: Develop a strong defense against narcissistic abuse by learning assertive communication and behavioral tools.
- **Reclaim**: Repel narcissists by developing a healthy sense of self-worth, setting boundaries, and taking control of your life narrative.

After a narcissist has been exposed, it is game over. Get ready to learn the psychological tools to outsmart narcissists and take back your power after surviving an abusive relationship.

Your healing journey starts now!

Part 1

RECOGNIZE

Understand Patterns of Narcissistic Abuse and
Manipulation Tactics Used to Psychologically
Break You Down

Chapter 1

You're Not Making Things Up—Something Is Off

"I am in love with you," I responded. He laughed the most beguiling and gentle laugh. "Of course you are," he replied. "I understand perfectly because I'm in love with myself."

–ANNE RICE

What Is a Gut Instinct?

Here's a fun fact: Your human gut is sometimes referred to as the *second brain* because it is a second hub for information. While it cannot think analytically or solve problems like your brain, its lining boasts over 100 million neurons that help with digestion, mood control, and alerting your brain of danger.

Can you think back to a past moment when you were overcome with fear and felt stomach cramps? Or maybe a period in your life when you were overwhelmed with stress and either lost your appetite or used food to numb your emotions? The common denominator in both of these experiences is your gut. That's right. The cramps, constipation, loss of appetite, or mood swings were information coming from your gut, not your brain.

Building on this foundation, a gut instinct can be described as internal intelligence that helps you make intuitive decisions about your life. Some may call it a sixth sense, which is information gathered intuitively, without relying on the five senses (i.e., sight, touch, hearing, smell, and taste). When you can quiet your mind long enough, your gut instinct naturally arises and guides you toward taking the correct action.

Some might wonder: *But how will I feel my gut instinct?* However, the better question to ask is: *How can I possibly miss it?*

If someone rearranged your bedroom, would you notice that something was different? Certainly, the changes would be so obvious that you would instinctively know someone had entered your room (even if you didn't have proof of it). When your gut instinct kicks in, it sends strong alerts throughout your body that are unmissable. You might label those alerts as anxiety or your imagination running wild, but the truth is you felt something—even without proof of where the feeling came from.

Moreover, your gut instinct might arise as a strong sense of right or wrong. Walking into a situation, you may instinctively know what feels good or harmful or when someone is a safe person to be around or a potential danger. Once again, your body sends unmissable alerts based on the information it is picking up from your environment or memories that have been triggered. For example, when you notice similar unhealthy patterns in a new partner that you have experienced from an ex-partner, your gut will caution you to be careful around them.

The most important thing to remember about your gut instinct is that it is not based on logical evidence. This means that when you often feel that something is right or wrong, you won't have the facts to support your intuition. The reason why this point is important to remember is that you will come across people in life who are masters at concealing their dark motives and may pretend to be someone they are not. Your gut will caution you about these people, but for the majority of the time, you won't have any proof to go by.

In these moments, trusting your gut instinct can be the best thing you can do for yourself. Don't wait for them to reveal their true colors before you start setting boundaries and taking the necessary steps to protect yourself. *If you sense that something is off about an individual, it probably is.*

The Difficulty of Trusting Your Gut

Mercy is a 32-year-old British traveler who went on a cross-country tour of the United States several years ago. At the midpoint of the trip, she decided to rent a car and go on a solo road trip through North Carolina. She had heard a lot about the scenic byways and stretches of mountains and ocean views and wanted to experience that for herself.

Unfortunately, she missed a turn and got lost along the way, so she stopped at a gas station to ask for directions. The gas station seemed closed because no other cars were in sight. However, a man was sitting under a covered area outside the small convenience shop. Mercy parked near the man and got out of her car. She explained that she was a traveler from the UK and didn't know where she was. The man seemed to be familiar with the area and knew where she was heading.

"Follow behind me with your car," he insisted, "I'll take you toward the nearest road exit, and you should be alright from there." Nothing about this plan raised any red flags for Mercy until she got in her car and started following the man. To this day, she cannot put her finger on what it was about him, his vehicle, or the plan that made her feel endangered. When they came near the road exit, a small voice inside her head said, "Continue driving straight. Don't make the turn."

She followed her instinct and continued to drive on the straight road. In her rearview mirror, she saw the man stop his car and make a U-turn. A sense of relief came over her. She intuitively knew that she was safe, and the threat was gone. A few miles ahead, she saw a small town and asked for directions to a coffee shop. It turns out that she was always on the right path toward her destination and taking that road exit would have taken her off the map completely.

In as much as your body warns you whenever you are in danger, you may sometimes misinterpret these alerts as your fears or wild thoughts. For instance, Mercy may have heard the small voice telling her to continue driving straight but told herself to stop being paranoid or judgmental of the man at the gas station. Or maybe, due to the lack of logical evidence about her gut instinct, she may have convinced herself to follow the man's plan.

Trusting your gut instinct isn't always easy when you are faced with situations that require informed decisions. The lack of concrete evidence makes it difficult for you to take those "hunches" seriously. Furthermore, if you don't have a lot of practice listening to your gut instinct, those body alerts can be interpreted negatively, such as being linked to anxiety or emotional triggers.

If you are prone to feeling anxious, trusting your gut instinct may sound like risky business. This is because that strong unshakeable feeling that something is off feels the same when you are worried or overthinking. Therefore, you may not always know whether what you are feeling is legitimate or a product of irrational thought. Additionally, anxiety activates your stress response, which sends your mind and body into overdrive. When you are functioning in overdrive, it can be difficult to think logically. Thus, the ideas or feelings you experience when your stress response is activated can easily be misinterpreted as your gut instinct, when, in fact, it isn't.

Besides fear and anxiety, another factor that can make it difficult to trust your gut instinct is a type of thinking error known as generalization. When you generalize, you assume that what happened in the past will repeat itself in the future. For example, if you have experienced losing your wallet when you go out at night, you might fear carrying a wallet due to thinking the same pattern will repeat itself. Or perhaps if you ordered a meal at a restaurant and got sick afterward, you may avoid going back to the restaurant because you don't trust the quality of its food.

When you generalize, what feels like your gut instinct could be your unresolved feelings about a past situation. The only way to avoid generalization is to process whatever hurt, failure, rejection, or disappointment you have experienced in the past so that you can approach current and future experiences with an open mind, free from any judgments.

Circling back to romantic relationships, trusting your gut can cause a lot of confusion, especially when your intuition picks up on information that contradicts the status quo of your relationship. Just imagine how confusing it would be to get a feeling that something is off with your new partner when they have been so kind and attentive toward you. Since what you see in front of you doesn't match what you are sensing intuitively, which reality are you supposed to believe?

To complicate this even further, carrying unresolved hurt from previous romantic relationships can make you doubt whether what you are sensing from your partner is truly your intuition or your trauma talking. This may lead to not taking any action at all out of fear of reacting to the wrong information. Alternatively, it may lead to confirmation bias, where you search for evidence that supports what you want to believe (i.e., that your new partner is a safe person and you have nothing to worry about) instead of weighing all of the information in front of you.

You are likely to come across these fears and doubts whenever you are presented with information and need to make decisions. The challenge for you will be learning to quiet your mind enough so you can sense your gut feelings. When your mind is on overdrive, it is hard to tell if what you are sensing is a stress response or a genuine gut instinct. Toward the end of the chapter, you will be presented with various mental and physical exercises that can calm your mind and help you tune in to your body.

Green Flags (and Red Flags) You Shouldn't Ignore in a Romantic Relationship

Trusting your gut instinct is extremely important when entering a romantic relationship since it involves intimacy and closeness. You want to ensure that you are opening up to a person who has your best interests at heart. However, with that said, not every *bad vibe* you pick up on is a cause for concern.

Remember, nobody is perfect, and there are going to be times of conflict and misunderstanding in your romantic relationships. Furthermore, based on the kind of childhood or relationship history your partner has, they may have bad habits that sometimes bring out the worst side of them. Yet still, this doesn't mean that they are a dangerous individual or that the relationship cannot work.

Your gut instinct is not supposed to be used as a tool to identify your likes and dislikes. Instead, it is meant to be a source of internal intelligence that you rely on when making critical decisions about your relationship like when to divulge personal information, how soon to become physically intimate with your partner, or whether you can trust them or not. Furthermore, your gut instinct won't only alert you of danger; at times, it can also indicate when something is good for you!

In this section, we will explore green and red flags you shouldn't ignore in a romantic relationship. Green flags refer to positive gut feelings that someone is good for you while red flags refer to negative gut feelings that someone may not be good for you. Please note that there are many other ways your intuition may speak to you, like having unexplained migraines or stomach cramps, seeing recurring symbols, or through synchronicities. Below are only eight examples of how your intuition shows you when someone is safe or unsafe to be around.

Red Flag: You Feel Nervous Constantly

Society often romanticizes getting butterflies in your stomach whenever you are with a significant other. However, they may not be a positive sign after all. Ongoing butterflies around your partner means that your body's nervous system cannot fully relax around them. In other words, something about how they behave or make you feel triggers your body's stress response. It may not be obvious what exactly makes you feel nervous about them, but slowing the relationship down would be necessary at this stage until you can reassess where you stand.

Green Flag: You Can Be Playful

Playfulness in a romantic relationship can indicate that you are in a safe environment. Examples of playful behaviors include telling jokes openly, trying new experiences together, being comfortable not looking your best, sharing embarrassing stories without fear of being judged, and being silly without feeling self-conscious. Being playful around your partner shows that you are comfortable being yourself. It takes a lot of courage to display your authentic self to someone else; however, it takes a secure person to accept you for who you are and not try to change you.

Red Flag: You Feel Tired Around Them

Your body learns to adapt to different surroundings to prepare for whatever may come. Feeling a wave of tiredness whenever you are with someone could mean they are draining your energy. Tiredness could also be a sign of boredom, disengagement, and being disconnected. Thus, if they are not emotionally draining your energy, you could have compatibility issues. In general, being with someone should make you feel energized and inspired instead of tired or bored.

Green Flag: You Are Connected

In a healthy romantic relationship, you don't have to force a connection. You are naturally drawn to your partner like a magnet and being around them feels good. They could be your complete opposite or share plenty of similarities, but what makes your relationship feel special is that you move in sync. Examples of connectedness in a romantic relationship include being able to anticipate your partner's needs, having stable and predictable routines, and knowing how to please your partner (and vice versa).

Red Flag: You Second-Guess Things You Didn't Previously

Being romantically involved with someone is supposed to make you a better version of yourself, not change who you are. The moment you start questioning things about yourself, try to trace where the doubts come from. For instance, have you doubted yourself for a while or have these feelings come during your relationship? Second-guessing yourself may also reveal signs of insecurities, such as not feeling good enough. If these insecurities were triggered recently, there could be behaviors occurring in your relationship that don't make you feel comfortable being your authentic self.

Green Flag: You Feel Comfortable Setting Boundaries

A clear sign that you are in a safe and healthy relationship is feeling confident saying no or expressing your limits. Your partner respectfully listens to you and takes your needs seriously instead of making you feel guilty for establishing rules or sharing different opinions from them. In a healthy relationship, setting boundaries does not cause physical discomfort or overthinking. It feels natural and nonthreatening, plus you don't fear that conflict will erupt afterward.

Red Flag: You Talk Yourself Into Staying

Relationships have highs and lows; however, you shouldn't reach a point where you need to convince yourself to stay. When there are sufficient red flags to justify why the relationship cannot work, take it as your intuition helping you to walk away. Ignoring your intuition doesn't make the dysfunction in the relationship disappear. It simply normalizes harmful behaviors that, in the worst-case scenario, could become abusive. You shouldn't need to make a case for staying with your partner. The reasons for being with them should be obvious for you and everyone else to see!

Green Flag: You Are Present

When you are in the company of a safe person, your mind stops racing between the past and future, and you can anchor yourself in the present moment. If you are prone to feeling anxious, you will notice that you spend less time overthinking when you are with your partner. In a healthy relationship, you are less worried about rushing to the next steps or achieving relationship milestones like moving in together or getting married. Even if you both aspire to reach those milestones, you are comfortable allowing plans to unfold naturally because every moment together brings joy.

Read over these green and red flags again to familiarize yourself with how your gut instinct manifests in romantic relationships. In healthy relationships, your gut instinct can show up as a deep sense of peace, but in unhealthy relationships, it can reveal itself as uneasiness.

Exercises to Connect to Your Gut Instinct and Tune In to Your Body

Earlier in the chapter, we explored several factors that make it difficult to trust your gut instinct. We mentioned how fear, anxiety, and past traumas can sometimes trigger the same warning signals passed by your gut, which makes it hard to tell whether what you are feeling is true or imagined. To increase sensitivity to your gut instinct, it is important to learn how to quiet your mind and tune in to your body.

The following mental and physical exercises are designed to manage irrational thinking, emotional triggers, and other mind games that can cloud your judgment and interfere with your intuition. If you have been diagnosed with a mental health disorder, consult your doctor before trying these exercises. For best results, practice these exercises when you are in a stable and calm state of mind.

Meditate

It is not easy to connect to your intuition when your mind is unsettled. Meditation is a therapeutic technique that slows down your mind and induces a state of relaxation in your body. The goal of meditation is to anchor your mind in the present moment and enhance your awareness of spontaneous thoughts, feelings, and sensations you are experiencing. It is common for people who practice meditation regularly to experience higher levels of creativity and self-awareness. In their meditative state of mind, they may easily pick up on intuitive thoughts and feelings too.

Get started: Practice a five-minute meditation, at least once a week, to calm your mind. Enter a quiet room in your house and sit down in a comfortable position. Gently close your eyes and begin to take slow and intentional breaths. Throughout your meditation, focus on your breathing. Notice the length, pace, rhythm, and movement of each breath. When you get distracted, gently refocus your attention on your breathing.

Complete a Body Scan

For many people, the gut instinct shows up as physical sensations. However, the lack of awareness or sensitivity to body sensations can cause some to miss or ignore their intuition. A body scan is a type of meditation exercise that can help you tune in to your body sensations and identify where discomfort is coming from and how intense it may feel. The more you practice body scans, the easier it will be for you to pinpoint what you are sensing and from where. Moreover, you may start to connect certain sensations with emotional messages, such as chest pains with rejection or stomach cramps with fear.

Get started: Lie down on a flat comfortable surface like a bed or patch of grass. Look up to the ceiling or sky and relax your body. Take a few deep breaths, then begin the body scan at the crown of your head. The aim is to scan each big muscle group (e.g., face, neck, shoulders, back, arms, chest) for any signs of tension or discomfort.

Spend at least two minutes calmly observing areas of tension around the muscle group before moving along. If you detect tension, explore how it feels and give it a rating out of 1-10 (10 being the highest level of intensity). Notice if any particular thoughts or feelings spontaneously come into your mind while observing the tension. If so, make a mental note of them. When the two minutes are up, move on to the next muscle group and complete another scan.

Spend Time Outdoors

Being outdoors is a great way to reconnect with your authentic self. Let's face it—there is something spiritual about being immersed in nature, breathing fresh air, listening to the sounds of birds, and absorbing the natural sunlight. There is also plenty of time and space to decompress and simply enjoy the present moment. In that relaxed and heightened state of awareness, your intuition can speak to you.

Get started: Plan an outdoor solo activity once a month. This could be a stroll in the park, hiking up a mountain, walking your dog, or swimming. Focus on being present and embrace the natural sounds and sights.

Take a Technology Detox

When consumed in excess, technology can be a distraction. It causes you to shift the focus away from your current physical, mental, and emotional state and preoccupy yourself with news, trends, and notifications from the external world. The danger of excessive technology consumption is that you may gradually become disconnected from yourself and your unique ideas, values, and beliefs. This means that instead of being guided by your intuition, your thoughts and feelings become largely influenced by the messages you absorb from the internet.

Get started: Dedicate one day a month to take a technology detox. Refrain from using your technological devices for 24 hours (or at least 12 hours). Find other ways to stimulate your mind, such as spending time outdoors, engaging in creative hobbies, or spending quality time with friends and family. If you cannot switch off your phone, for whatever reason, close your apps and put the phone on silent. Whenever you feel the urge to browse through your notifications, get up and take a walk or complete a house chore.

Journal

Journaling is a therapeutic technique that can be turned into a stimulating hobby. The purpose of journaling is to offload everything on your mind so that you can observe, analyze, and draw patterns from your thoughts. The practice of journaling increases self-awareness and enables you to connect the dots and make sense of what you are thinking or feeling about a situation. As a result, you can identify signs and coincidences that can shift your perspective.

Get started: Purchase a pen and notebook dedicated to journaling about your romantic relationships. Throughout the stages of getting to know someone, document your thoughts and feelings. Your journal entries don't have to be based on a specific topic; you are free to write as much as you like about anything that comes to your mind. Nonetheless, if you could benefit from structure and guidance, use the following journal prompts as inspiration:

1. What do you value in a romantic partner?
2. How do you express love to others?
3. How do you desire to be shown love?
4. Do you feel worthy of being loved?
5. What do you think draws people to you?
6. What does a healthy relationship look like?
7. What does an unhealthy relationship look like?
8. How well do you express your needs in a relationship?
9. Describe a time when you felt safe with a significant other.
10. Describe a time when your intuition warned you about a significant other.

Chapter 2

Call It What It Is: Narcissistic Abuse

The narcissist is like a bucket with a hole in the bottom: No matter how much you put in, you can never fill it up. The phrase "I never feel like I am enough" is the mantra of the person in a narcissistic relationship.

–RAMANI DURVASULA

The Monster in My Bed

Veronica met her ex-husband Hunter when she was 23 years old. At the time, he was 15 years older than her and had a stable career and life. She got pregnant at 24, and they married a year later.

Hunter's behavior toward Veronica changed after they married and moved in with each other. She noticed that he seemed less patient with her but assumed that it was due to the arrival of the new baby. However, months went by, and Hunter kept becoming progressively nasty and controlling.

He blamed their lack of intimacy on her and said she no longer excited him. He began going out on weekends without her and made her feel guilty whenever she planned nights out with her girlfriends. Despite his coldness toward his wife, he was extremely possessive of her. He always wanted to know her whereabouts and who she was talking to because, in his mind, she was capable of cheating on him.

The only real power he had over her was that he controlled the finances at home. After becoming pregnant at a young age and getting married soon after, Veronica became a stay-at-home mom. Hunter used his financial power to control what she could access and what decisions she could make. The day she decided to get a part-time job was the day she started to win her life back. Making her own money gave her a sense of achievement, *a feeling that she was good enough*.

As time went by, she accepted full-time positions and became a busy professional woman. She had saved enough money to move out of her double-story home and find a decent apartment for her and her child. The divorce papers came later once she had settled into her new life and got to marinate in the newfound freedom. Veronica continues to attend therapy and maintains a tight-knit community of friends and family who love her dearly. When it comes to her dating life, she is open to meeting eligible bachelors who are not threatened by a woman who knows her worth!

What Is Narcissistic Abuse?

Narcissistic abuse is a type of abuse that is caused by narcissistic behaviors. It is often perpetuated by some people (but not all) who suffer from narcissistic personality disorder (NPD). We can define NPD as a condition where the sufferer needs excessive admiration to the extent of building a grandiose self-image and lacking empathy for others.

Narcissistic abuse can take on different forms, such as having components of verbal, emotional, or physical abuse. It can be public for everybody to see or disguised as passive-aggressive and manipulative behaviors. But regardless of how the abuse is dressed up, it is still psychologically damaging to those who are affected by it.

The difficulty in identifying narcissistic abuse is that not everyone with NPD behaves the same way. For example, one narcissistic person might be obsessed with the spotlight and become noticeably frustrated when they are ignored. Another narcissistic person might avoid the spotlight at all costs and prefer to convey a sense of righteousness and being devoted to the welfare of others.

To see the many sides of narcissistic abuse, explore the following three types of narcissism and learn how they can be displayed in relationships.

Overt Narcissism

Overt narcissism, also known as grandiose narcissism, seeks public recognition and admiration from others. This type of narcissistic individual believes there is something special about who they are that makes them superior to others. As a result, they tend to display a lack of empathy and a sense of entitlement in relationships. Typical forms of abuse associated with this type of narcissism are exploitation.

Covert Narcissism

Not every narcissistic person has a larger-than-life personality. Some prefer to not be exposed for who they are and what their motives are. They are known as covert narcissists because their forms of manipulation are not obvious. Nevertheless, this doesn't make their behaviors less damaging. Typical forms of abuse associated with covert narcissism are avoidant behaviors, playing the victim, and gaslighting.

Malignant Narcissism

At an extreme level, narcissism can become dangerous and turn into malignant narcissism. This form of narcissism can be aggressive and take extreme measures to achieve motives. For example, if a malignant narcissist is after power at work, they are willing to sabotage coworkers or steal money. In relationships, they can be abusive by taking pleasure in inflicting emotional or physical pain and making their loved ones suffer.

Breaking Down the Narcissistic Abuse Cycle

Even though narcissistic abuse takes different forms, there is a common pattern of manipulation that narcissistic people use to keep their victims trapped in an ongoing cycle of abuse. This is referred to as the narcissistic abuse cycle and can be broken down into three stages.

Stage 1: Idealization

When a narcissist first meets you, they put you on a pedestal. You might feel like the first woman they have ever truly loved because of the amount of praise and admiration they show you. Moreover, due to their ability to read people, they might pick up on your insecurities and find ways of celebrating them and making you feel beautiful.

A clear sign that you are being idealized is that the attention given to you can feel overwhelming. Just imagine going from having a normal dating life with a regular guy to having flowers delivered to your house every week, extravagant dates, and surprise vacations to places you have always dreamed of going. As much as you may enjoy being pampered in this way, on an instinctual level, you know that it isn't natural.

A second sign of idealization is noticing the relationship progressing at a rapid speed. For example, you meet the individual this week, next

week you are having sleepovers, and the following wee
introduced to their siblings. Once again, this m
everything you would hope for, but on an instinctual l
that it isn't natural.

The dark side of being idealized is that the narcissistic individual starts
to invade your life, intentionally takes up most of your time, and
imposes their values and expectations on you. If you were someone
who enjoyed girl time with your friends, for example, you may rarely
see them once your narcissistic partner swoops in and takes over your
calendar.

Stage 2: Devaluation

Narcissists tend to use up all of their energy deposits during the
idealization stage. After a few months of treating you like a queen and
promising the world, they begin to reveal their true colors. The
devaluation stage officially begins when the narcissistic individual
shows you another side to them. This could be a lazy, disrespectful,
aggressive, or controlling side that you didn't know existed.

Since the contrast between who they appeared to be in the beginning
and who they are now is so large, it is normal for you to ignore the red
flags or make excuses for their unpleasant behaviors. For example,
when your partner makes hurtful comments about you, you may
blame it on alcohol or stress at work and shrug it off. The denial about
their behavior may continue until an outsider points it out to you.

Being devalued is painful because not only are you removed from the
pedestal, but you are treated worse than a stranger. Verbal and
emotional abuse is always unwarranted and never a true reflection of
who you are and what you are worth. Part of the reason why a
narcissist will treat you so poorly is to lower your expectations from

.ne relationship so that you stop requiring them to be the gentleman, provider, and protector whom you fell in love with. They want to psychologically wear you out to the point where you feel appreciative of the little they do whenever they feel like it.

Stage 3: Rejection

Narcissistic individuals do not feel remorse for taking their victims through the devaluation stage and treating them poorly. Many of them may never come to accept responsibility for the hurt they have caused others. The final stage of the narcissistic abuse cycle is rejection, and this is where your narcissistic partner shifts the blame for the dysfunctional relationship onto you. In other words, they attempt to make you feel responsible for the problems you are facing in the relationship.

Rejection may not always come in the form of breaking up with you. Many narcissistic people thrive in relationships (even dysfunctional ones) because they receive some form of validation or control from their loved ones. Therefore, even when a narcissistic partner rejects you, the last thing they will think of is leaving. This means that rejection will likely come in other forms, such as living separate lives, cheating and having affairs, threatening to end the relationship, or feeling contempt toward you.

It is usually very difficult for victims to leave the relationship once they have been rejected. They may suffer from extremely low self-esteem and self-worth and cannot imagine being happy outside of the relationship. Additionally, they may fear the narcissistic partner's rage or capacity to inflict harm if they do decide to leave. What they don't realize is that the narcissistic partner is powerless and only *projects* an image of power.

The purpose of this book is to show you that it is possible to break free from the narcissistic abuse cycle and either separate yourself from your narcissistic partner or set boundaries to regain a sense of power in the relationship. However, it is important to remember that breaking free from narcissistic abuse doesn't mean you can change a narcissistic person. Only they can change themselves if they choose to heal.

How Doctors Diagnose NPD

NPD is a mental health disorder recognized in the fifth edition of the American Psychiatric Association's *Diagnostic and Statistical Manual of Mental Disorders (DSM-5)*. To receive a diagnosis, the first step is for people who display narcissistic behaviors to seek help. Due to the nature of the condition, many people with narcissism do not feel there is anything wrong with them. Thus, there is a larger number of undiagnosed narcissistic people than those who are in treatment and address their behavioral issues.

Two important types of doctors who specialize in treating personality disorders like narcissism are psychologists and psychiatrists. Both doctors are trained to evaluate a patient's psychological state of mind; however, the difference is that a psychologist will often recommend psychotherapy as a treatment option while a psychiatrist will prescribe medication.

During the medical exam, the chosen doctor will go through the DSM-5 assessment criteria and determine how many of the symptoms of NPD the patient displays. To be diagnosed with NPD, the patient must exhibit at least five out of the nine criteria. The nine criteria are as follows (Ambardar, 2021):

1. A grandiose sense of self-importance.

2. Being preoccupied with illusions of infinite power, success, beauty, or ideal love.

3. The belief that he or she is gifted and can only be understood (or should only associate with) other gifted people.

4. The need for continuous and excessive admiration.

5. A sense of entitlement.

6. A lack of empathy.

7. Evidence of interpersonal exploitive behaviors.

8. Extreme envy of others or believing that others are envious of him or her.

9. Evidence of haughty and arrogant behaviors or attitudes.

The doctor may also ask questions about the patient's medical history, interpersonal relationships, and childhood upbringing to identify contributing factors to their mental and emotional well-being as well as to rule out co-occurring conditions like chronic anxiety or depression, substance use disorder (SUD), bipolar personality disorder (BPD), or antisocial personality disorder (ASPD).

There is a misconception that NPD cannot be cured but that simply isn't true. What often makes NPD seem incurable is the fact that many who suffer from the disorder do not seek treatment. Without going through the healing journey, narcissism cannot be treated. Several types of psychotherapy can address symptoms of narcissism. These include cognitive behavioral therapy (CBT), dialectical behavioral therapy (DBT), metacognitive therapy, trauma counseling, and couples or family therapy.

Currently, no medication treats NPD. However, psychiatrists will prescribe various medications to address symptoms of underlying conditions patients are living with. For example, those who display symptoms of anxiety and depression will be prescribed antidepressants or antianxiety medications. If they display symptoms of bipolar or paranoia, they can be prescribed antipsychotic or anticonvulsant medications.

Lastly, even though narcissistic behaviors may seem premeditated sometimes, many people show signs of NPD who may not be aware of it. NPD can go under the radar for many years and only fully reveal itself when a major crisis erupts in the individual's life.

For instance, there are many stories of women (and men) who dated and even went on to marry narcissistic partners and didn't see any signs of their disorder until a major transition occurred in their lives or relationships. The narcissistic individual may have lost his job, lost a loved one, or been diagnosed with a chronic illness that affected their ability to live independently. These highly stressful circumstances can trigger dormant symptoms of NPD and turn a seemingly good person into a monster.

Who Are Narcissists Attracted to?

If you have encountered a narcissistic individual in the dating scene, you may have wondered: *Why me? What did this male or female predator see in me that made them pursue me?*

To understand the perfect partner for a narcissist, you must understand their motivations for seeking romantic partnerships in the first place. Someone with NPD has trouble empathizing with others. They also tend to be self-absorbed and care about fulfilling their needs and comforts. Their motivations for pursuing a love interest are to satisfy their needs and receive endless amounts of adoration or empowerment. Therefore, they are more likely to be attracted to people who demonstrate a willingness to take care of them.

You might be wondering how important physical appearances are to people with NPD. The answer depends on what type of narcissistic individual you are speaking to. For example, an overt or grandiose narcissist cares a lot about their image and status and, therefore, feels attraction for people who are extremely beautiful, successful, and well-known in their circles.

In contrast, someone with overt narcissism may not be as superficial in comparison. What they are mostly interested in is finding a partner who they can control. Thus, they tend to date different types of people and don't put too much emphasis on external appearances.

With that said, a person's character is the most important for a narcissist when choosing a romantic partner. They often date or marry someone who displays specific personality traits and behaviors that make it easier for them to be deceived and manipulated. Let's take a look at some examples of personality traits that draw a narcissistic individual toward a specific person.

Self-Sacrificing

A narcissist is drawn to someone who finds pleasure in taking care of others and doesn't have clear limits about how much they can give. They find people-pleasers and codependent people particularly attractive because, in exchange for giving them the partnership they want, the narcissist receives endless amounts of validation and admiration. Another benefit of being with a self-sacrificing partner is that they tend to feel uncomfortable expressing their needs or demanding the same kind of attentiveness in return. A narcissistic individual may pretend to be generous and responsive to their partner's needs during the idealization stage, but this act doesn't last very long.

Strong-Willed

There is a myth that a narcissist goes for a weak and vulnerable person. However, this isn't true. Believe it or not, a narcissistic individual loves a challenge because, in the pursuit of a strong-willed person, they gain status and feel more powerful. The type of catch for a narcissist is someone who is admired by others and displays character strengths like being assertive and confident. The motivation for pursuing such a person is to either feel special being associated with them or feel incredibly powerful when they can psychologically break them down.

Insecure

Before a narcissist decides to pursue someone, they will look for chinks in their armor that could be used as leverage later on in the relationship when the devaluation process starts. For example, a narcissistic individual would rather date or marry someone who is insecure or living with unresolved trauma than someone who is on a healing journey and has heightened self-awareness. At the beginning of the relationship, they will pretend to show sympathy for their partner's psychological issues; however, later on, these same issues are targeted and exploited to pull them down.

Empathetic

A common trick used by a narcissist to manipulate someone is playing the victim card. They purposefully attempt to appear weak so that they can receive attention and validation. Empaths have a built-in savior complex and feel fulfilled whenever they can put out another person's fire. Due to their increased level of sensitivity, they may take on the suffering of a loved one and feel responsible for providing support. An empath may get worn out from constantly hearing and solving the narcissist's problems, but unlike other people, they may find it difficult to set firm boundaries and learn when to say no.

Self-Sufficient

A narcissistic individual is drawn to a self-sufficient go-getter who lives an independent lifestyle. They find such a person attractive because they tend to be mature and willing to handle real-life problems like paying the bills and taking care of the household. Around a self-sufficient person, a narcissist doesn't have to carry any significant responsibility. This affirms their belief of being special and superior to others. On the other hand, they may compete with their self-sufficient partner or find ways to devalue them so that they can maintain a sense of control in the relationship.

Can you start to see a pattern in the type of people a narcissist is drawn to? If we were to summarize their ideal man or woman, it would be someone who is strong and capable but has character flaws like being insecure, self-sacrificing, or overly empathetic. These character flaws, combined with a lack of healthy limits or boundaries, make them easy to manipulate.

The Long-Term Consequences of Staying in an Abusive Relationship

Even if you feel strong enough to defend yourself against a narcissistic partner, no type of abuse is acceptable.

It is important not to think of a narcissistic partner's behaviors as being "bad habits" but to see them as a form of abuse. What's worse is that their reluctance to accept accountability makes it impossible to address the abuse and root it out of your relationship.

Furthermore, since narcissistic abuse occurs in a cycle, there is an aspect of it that is calculated and premeditated. For instance, very early on in a relationship, a narcissistic partner knows they intend to control or manipulate you. The deceitful nature of a narcissist makes them an unsafe person to be around. In other words, they make decisions without your best interests at heart.

You may not see the consequences of narcissistic abuse immediately because many times the damage is done on a psychological level. However, this doesn't mean that you are immune to the long-term psychological repercussions of staying in an abusive relationship. Like any abuse, narcissistic abuse affects not only your love life but also your health, career, finances, spirituality, and ability to build positive relationships.

Some of the common trauma symptoms you may experience after months or years of narcissistic abuse include:

- anxiety
- depression
- unwanted thoughts
- suicidal thoughts
- nightmares and flashbacks
- post-traumatic stress disorder (PTSD)

Narcissistic abuse can also change how you see yourself and how you interact with the world. It significantly lowers your self-esteem to the extent of making you feel worthless. If you were a bubbly and confident person before you met the narcissistic individual, you may look in the mirror and see a person plagued with insecurities and haunted by their inner critical thoughts. What makes narcissistic abuse so dangerous is that instead of turning against your abuser, it forces you to turn against yourself.

The good news is that help is available. Narcissistic abuse is not a death sentence. The moment you recognize the signs of abuse and an unstable partner, you can seek support and guidance from a community of experts, doctors, and survivors who are willing to accept you with open arms!

Types of Support Available for Survivors of Narcissistic Abuse

Being in an abusive relationship can be a lonely experience, especially when you have been isolated from your community. It is important to reach out to others to receive strength from your community and realize that you are not alone.

When you get in touch with a community of others who have experienced narcissistic abuse, you gain access to more information about NPD. This is a great way to make sense of narcissistic abuse and understand the complex dynamic of your romantic relationship. Moreover, having more information at your disposal empowers you to make more informed and strategic decisions about your life as well as your next steps.

Besides reconnecting with friends and family, there is professional support available both virtually and in person. The two types of support we will look at below are narcissistic abuse support groups and narcissistic abuse therapy.

Narcissistic Abuse Support Groups

Narcissistic abuse support groups are safe online or in-person communities consisting of survivors of narcissistic abuse. Some groups may be peer-led, while a trained therapist or coach may lead others. When joining a narcissistic abuse support group, you don't need to fear that what you share with other members will be leaked or used against you later. Confidentiality and respect for members' contributions are part of what makes the group feel supportive and validating.

Sharing your unique experiences is not a prerequisite for joining a narcissistic abuse support group. The mere fact that you are open to learning about narcissism is enough reason to attend meetings and listen to the discussions taking place. Nevertheless, if you are looking for a safe space to express your thoughts and feelings, you are encouraged to speak up without fear of judgment or retaliation.

Joining a narcissistic abuse support group is the right move for you if you are ready to confront the issues experienced in your relationship but not yet ready to explore formal counseling options. Perhaps at this stage of your healing journey, you are looking for like-minded people to provide social support. You may also be someone who is opposed to therapy and prefers to have real discussions with people who have been in your shoes and have freed themselves from narcissistic abuse.

To find a narcissistic abuse support group near you, ask for referrals from a nearby mental health clinic or general hospital. Alternatively, you can visit a domestic violence center and inquire about the type of support groups they offer. Many domestic violence centers offer support groups for survivors of intimate partner violence (IPV) and narcissistic abuse falls under this large umbrella category. If you are looking for reliable groups online, browse through the Good Therapy website and search for support groups based on your state. Good Therapy serves as a great resource to find different treatment options for narcissistic abuse, such as counseling, telehealth, and residential treatment centers.

Below are additional resources and groups available to you:

- **Al-Anon**: A 12-step program for friends and family members of alcoholics. In this safe space, you get to connect with other families who are dealing with the pain of addiction and receive the support and information to cope with your reality.
- **National Domestic Violence Hotline**: If you are feeling unsafe in your relationships, this organization provides a hotline, online chat, and text line to reach out for help. Their website also includes useful resources and a directory for support groups.
- **Help Within Reach**: Started by therapist Pam Raphael, this organization offers a variety of narcissistic abuse support groups that meet online and are open to people from across the world.
- **I Believe Your Abuse**: An online website that provides plenty of information about NPD and offers counseling and free support groups for people within and outside the US.

Narcissistic Abuse Therapy

For more practical tools and strategies to recover from narcissistic abuse, you may want to consider going to therapy. You may have your personal views about therapy based on what you have heard or experienced in the past. However, I would encourage you to be open-minded when exploring therapy options since not every therapist or treatment is the same.

Finding the right type of therapy is winning half of the battle. That is why doctors have created a specific category of therapy for survivors of narcissistic abuse. The purpose of narcissistic abuse therapy is to help you understand the impact and effects of being exposed to someone with NPD. You get to learn the psychology of narcissism so you can make sense of your relationship experiences.

Moreover, narcissistic therapy guides you through the process of healing by introducing you to various forms of psychotherapy and equipping you with the tools to build a strong sense of self and protect yourself against any forms of abuse in the future.

The following therapies are recommended for survivors of narcissistic abuse:

- **one-on-one narcissistic abuse therapy**: Individual online or in-person therapy sessions with a professional narcissistic abuse therapist.
- **group therapy for narcissistic abuse**: Online or in-person group therapy sessions where survivors of narcissistic abuse are counseled by a therapist or coach and undergo a shared healing journey.
- **cognitive behavioral therapy**: A form of psychotherapy that focuses on helping survivors of narcissistic abuse recognize and replace negative thought patterns, emotions, and behaviors within themselves so they can develop a positive self-concept and manage self-critical thoughts and triggers.
- **trauma-informed therapy**: A treatment option that helps survivors process and heal from the trauma caused by narcissistic abuse. Various mind techniques and therapies are used to regulate the nervous system, release stored trauma and tension, and promote healing on a physiological level.
- **dialectical behavioral therapy**: A form of psychotherapy that combines individual therapy sessions, group skills training, and coaching. This therapy aims to help survivors

cope with highly stressful life situations by teaching them how to practice mindfulness, emotional regulation, distress tolerance, and interpersonal effectiveness skills.

The goal of narcissistic abuse therapy is to empower you with knowledge and tools to recognize signs of abuse, learn positive coping mechanisms, and develop a strong sense of self-worth. The focus is not on changing your partner but on deepening the relationship you have with yourself. In the second and third parts of the book, you will be introduced to concepts and skills often taught in therapy rooms. While the information will be valuable, it does not substitute seeking professional counseling for narcissistic abuse.

Chapter 3

Meet the Person Behind the Charm

When I look at narcissism through the vulnerability lens, I see the shame-based fear of being ordinary. I see the fear of never feeling extraordinary enough to be noticed, to be lovable, to belong, or to cultivate a sense of purpose.

– BRENÉ BROWN

Going Back to the Narcissist's Childhood

To understand who narcissists truly are, we have to explore their pasts and attempt to connect the dots of how they became these unfeeling individuals.

So, what went so wrong in the narcissistic individual's past for them to become who they are today?

The best place to start is in their early childhood. Experts say that within the first five to seven years of life, a child will learn cues and behavioral patterns from their environment to make sense of the world. On an instinctual level, this is the child's way of learning acceptable and unacceptable behaviors to protect themselves against harm.

An adult narcissist often is raised in a dysfunctional household where there isn't enough stability and structure for the child to find their balance, develop positive self-esteem, and feel confident exploring the world. They might be raised by abusive, neglectful, or dismissive parents who may or may not live with a mental health condition or substance abuse problem.

For a great portion of their childhood, the child finds themselves in very unsafe, unpredictable, and traumatic situations. They feel immensely vulnerable as a result of not receiving the protection and consistent nurturing from their parents. Eventually, they may develop unhealthy coping mechanisms to regulate their bodies and adapt to their unstable environment. Narcissistic tendencies emerge as a psychological defense against the physical, mental, and emotional abuse they are exposed to.

It is worth going deeper and exploring the role of parents in raising adult narcissists. A child who is raised by a parent who lacks empathy and shows a lack of responsiveness to their needs may grow up disconnected from their thoughts and feelings. Outwardly, they may appear strong and resilient, but inwardly they feel hollow and lonely. To impress and connect with their parent, they may develop a fake persona that appeals to their parent's needs and desires. If this fake persona is accepted, the child learns to reject their authentic self and become someone else to maintain social connections with others.

A narcissist will go to great lengths to hide the deep-rooted sense of shame and worthlessness they feel. If we were to trace where these strong emotions stem from, we would be taken back into their childhood. The truth is that like anybody with a troubled upbringing, a narcissist carries unresolved emotional wounds. The difference, however, is that they tend to internalize their negative experiences and grow to resent who they are.

For instance, they may look down upon themselves for being bullied as a child, being raised in an impoverished background, or going through many life challenges to succeed. Some may feel like failures for not being smart at school, achieving status symbols, or making their parents proud. The common theme is self-blame, and to feel better about themselves, the only option is to disconnect from their reality and live in a state of disillusionment.

The world that a narcissist recreates for themselves is one where they can escape the feeling of not being good enough. In this utopian world, they are the smartest and most admirable person alive. They are bestowed a god-like status and believe they should be given special treatment. Of course, this is a fantasy and extreme exaggeration of real life; however, for someone who grew up abused or traumatized, this utopian world provides relief from an unkind and dangerous world.

Since narcissism is a personality disorder, an adult narcissist struggles with identity issues that stem from unresolved childhood neglect and trauma. The biggest challenge though is that due to disconnecting from their authentic self at an early age, it is difficult for an adult narcissist to admit they have lost touch with who they are and need help to heal from deep-rooted shame and sense of worthlessness. Some adult narcissists may have even forgotten traumatic events or periods of their childhood or may avoid any topics that take them back to painful moments from the past.

While we tend to demonize adult narcissists for plausible reasons, inside each one of them is a disturbed child whose only option for survival back then was to turn inward and cut off from reality.

How Narcissists Perceive the World and Others

Narcissistic individuals are plagued with fears and insecurities. They believe the world is a dangerous place full of manipulators and opportunists. Once again, this worldview is informed by their troubled past where they were harmed, rejected, and betrayed by the people they trusted most.

To survive in the world, narcissists believe that they must outsmart others to maintain a sense of control and avoid being hurt. The main motive for forming relationships with others is to fulfill their needs and reduce feelings of vulnerability. They display a sense of entitlement, believing that they deserve to be treated well. However, the double standard is that they don't feel obliged to treat others well. The only person they care about is themselves, and they will go to extreme lengths to make sure they are safe and secure—even if it means inflicting pain on others.

The Zero-Sum Game: Narcissists in Romantic Relationships

Narcissistic people have a strong and deep distrust of others, even their blood relatives. They have seen and experienced the worst side of life and subsequently lost faith in the goodness of mankind. The inability to trust and see the good in others makes narcissists skeptical and apathetic lovers.

When they come across kind-hearted and compassionate people in the dating scene, they see easy targets to manipulate. Kindness and compassion, to them, are seen as character flaws or foolish behavior. They cannot imagine how someone can desire to help and support others without seeking anything in return. Once upon a time, narcissists were kind-hearted and compassionate children too.

However, they got burned several times for being that way and decided that arrogance and aggressiveness were better traits to adopt.

The positive emotions and behaviors exhibited by narcissists at the beginning of a romantic relationship are put on. They have studied human nature long enough to know that people generally gravitate toward likable people. If they revealed their cold and selfish nature upfront, nobody would desire to be with them and that would trigger rejection and abandonment wounds. Thus, their charm, charisma, and seduction are learned behaviors to make unsuspecting victims fall in love with them.

Romantic relationships are seen as a zero-sum game to narcissists: There must be a winner and a loser—and they certainly won't be the loser. Manipulation and deception are used as tools to create a power imbalance in their relationships, where they have more control and authority than their significant other. Being superior to their partners is important to narcissists because that prevents them from feeling vulnerable to rejection or a sense of powerlessness. They must always have some type of advantage over their partners whether it is having more beauty, social status, or economic power.

Nevertheless, there isn't enough power to make narcissists feel secure in themselves or in their romantic relationships. What they don't realize is that the root cause of feeling powerless is internal not external. Therefore, even when they have full control over their relationships, they continue to feel insecure and inferior to their counterparts. As a result, narcissistic individuals must inflict emotional pain on their partners to prove to themselves continuously that they are smarter, stronger, and have the upper hand.

The desire to hurt their loved ones can be obsessive and lead to the worst kinds of abuse. They tend to play experimental games on their partners to test how far they can hurt them before they break down. Malignant narcissists, who are the most dangerous type of narcissists, get a sense of pleasure in causing their loved ones emotional distress. Their sadistic behaviors stem from being tormented by their own sense of inadequacy and emptiness. In other words, since they are cut off from their own emotions, hurting others allows them to feel something—in most cases, pleasure. But unfortunately, hurting others only brings temporary satisfaction and doesn't bring an end to their ongoing internal conflict.

Lastly, narcissistic individuals use romantic relationships for what is known as "narcissistic supply." Partners help them fill an inner void and mirror the qualities they cannot connect to within themselves. For example, having a generous partner makes them feel worthy of having their needs met and a responsible partner makes them feel secure in themselves. Without the constant outpouring of love and validation, narcissists would have no other choice but to confront their inner demons. Therefore, they need the distraction from romantic relationships to avoid feeling hollow and empty.

Narcissists are also prone to cheating and having countless affairs. This is because attention from one person isn't enough to fill the inner void. In most cases, when the "honeymoon stage" of a relationship is over (about three months into getting to know someone), they start to look for new romances elsewhere and continue going through a series of honeymoon stages. With that said, narcissists are unlikely to leave romantic partnerships even when the love has waxed cold. For them, having somebody is better than not having anyone at all. Their deep-rooted abandonment issues won't allow them to let go of anyone. It is normally the abused significant other who decides to walk away.

Can Narcissists Fall in Love?

A question that many survivors of narcissistic abuse ask themselves is whether or not their narcissistic partners truly loved them. They wrestle with their reality trying to figure out if what they felt from their partner was genuine or superficial all along.

There isn't a direct answer to this question because while narcissists are capable of loving others, their understanding of love is distorted. To make this point more clear, let's travel back into an adult narcissist's past and examine how love was shown to them by their parents. In many instances, love was not displayed in healthy and positive ways. It may have come with conditions, used as a reward for good behavior, or used as a weapon to exploit.

An adult narcissist, therefore, has some understanding of what love is, but it isn't anything healthy that promotes safe and reciprocal relationships. For them, love is a tool used to get what they want from their significant other. For example, if they need to express affection and be attentive to gain their partner's trust at the beginning of a relationship, that is exactly what they will do. Their loving acts do not come from a sincere place, which explains why they are unable to maintain the same loving behaviors in the long term.

Several factors make it difficult for a narcissistic individual to genuinely fall in love. First, true love is self-sacrificing. It requires couples to suspend their needs and respond to those of their significant others, and vice versa. This dance between couples is what ensures that both of them feel fulfilled in their relationships. A narcissist is too emotionally fragile to think of anyone besides themselves. Thus, in relationships, they tend to either be transactional (i.e. you help me and I'll help you) or self-serving.

Second, true love requires a willingness to grow and learn habits and behaviors that compromise the quality of your relationship. This type of mentality is known as a growth mindset and describes an openness to feedback and continuous learning. Loving relationships are formed by two imperfect people who are willing to grow with each other and become better versions of themselves. A narcissist believes they are already the best version of themselves. They are unable to adopt a growth mindset because that would threaten their perception of being perfect. Their utopian world is built on the idea that they don't need to change, others do.

Third, true love requires vulnerability—something that is considered a weakness to a narcissist. Because they see romantic partners as targets to be manipulated, they are unable to let their guard down in front of them. In some cases, particularly during the idealization stage, a narcissist may pretend to open up and show vulnerability. This is a calculated move to lower their partner's psychological defense and gain the upper hand early on. Other instances when a narcissist may show vulnerability are when they are losing an argument, have been caught in a lie, or fear that their partner is planning on leaving them.

The inability to experience or show genuine love can be a haunting reality for some narcissistic people who have some level of self-awareness. This is often the case when they meet kind-hearted people who have pure intentions to love them. Receiving so much love and knowing they are incapable of reciprocating the same feelings can be devastating. Think of the Disney fairytale *Beauty and the Beast*, where the beast only became conscious of his identity when he met a princess who saw the potential for good in him.

This haunting realization is the turning point for a few narcissists. For the majority, it is simply the point at which they decide to break up with the good person or find additional sources of narcissistic supply who will provide a much-needed distraction from looking deep inside of themselves. In other words, instead of turning to healing, they become avoidant and detached.

Chapter 4

Dark and Dangerous Psychological Tactics to Be Aware of

Intuition—once you have had a narcissist in your life, you must develop your intuition and learn to listen to it and act accordingly.

–TRACY MALONE

What Is Psychological Manipulation?

A narcissist doesn't look dangerous when you first meet them. They are masters at creating illusions and coming across like any typical man or woman you might be attracted to. They might have a stable job, hobbies, and a circle of friends, which makes them appear to be grounded and level-headed.

However, underneath the facade is a predator looking for a more narcissistic supply. Since being direct about their motives wouldn't get them what they want, they have to lie and cheat to achieve their goals. They use emotional weapons instead of physical ones, making their violence seem unplanned. As the person on the receiving end, you may start to doubt your instincts and wonder if what you are sensing is real or imaginary.

What makes narcissistic abuse harmful is that it doesn't leave physical scars. As a result, there is no physical evidence to prove that you have been violated. A narcissist will use what is called psychological manipulation to bypass your mental and emotional defenses and control how you think, feel, and engage with the world.

Psychological manipulation describes the act of controlling another person's emotional state through coercion or persuasion. It is considered a form of emotional abuse and can severely damage the victim's ability to trust, develop a strong sense of self, and build healthy relationships. Ongoing psychological manipulation can lead to chronic mental health conditions like generalized anxiety disorder (GAD), post-traumatic stress disorder (PTSD), depression, and substance abuse issues.

Like many behaviors displayed by a narcissist, psychological manipulation is typically something they learn from childhood. For instance, they may have been raised by an abusive parent who used psychological manipulation tactics against them, or they may have taught themselves these tactics as a defense mechanism to feel protected against the violence in their household or community.

Narcissists are not ignorant of the damage caused by psychological manipulation. They are aware of the long-term effects of continuous emotional violence and continue to hurt others anyway. Overt and covert narcissists may justify their behaviors by saying, "I need to do whatever I have to do to get what I want," whereas malignant narcissists might justify their behaviors by saying, "If you are foolish enough to let me manipulate you, then you deserve it!"

Psychological Manipulation Tactics to Be Aware of

If psychological manipulation could be spotted easily, many narcissists wouldn't be able to get away with hurting others. This type of weapon is deliberately subtle, passive-aggressive, and confusing.

Psychological manipulation aims to get the victim to second-guess their thoughts and feelings and disconnect with their sense of reality. This creates an opening for the narcissist to swoop in and plant seeds of toxic beliefs and emotions in their mind. Over time, the victim's psychological defenses break down and they start to accept their new controlled reality.

To protect yourself from psychological manipulation, it is important to learn various tactics used by narcissists to inflict mental and emotional harm. When you are aware of these tactics, it becomes easier to trust your gut instinct when you sense manipulation taking place in your relationships.

Consider the following common psychological manipulation tactics.

Gaslighting

Gaslighting is the act of making someone doubt what they believe to be true. It involves intentionally distorting reality to make the other person question their opinions, values, memory, and sense of identity. The ultimate goal is to make the victim doubt themselves and rely on the narcissist's version of what is real and what is not.

Examples of gaslighting include being told that your recollection of past events isn't accurate, being told repeatedly that you are mentally unstable or paranoid, and being made to feel responsible for your partner's wrong actions.

Gaslighting may sound like:

- "You don't make any sense right now."
- "You're too sensitive."
- "Why are you so paranoid?"
- "I'm sorry if you feel that way."
- "You know I wouldn't intentionally do that to hurt you."

Triangulation

Triangulation occurs when a third party is brought into a conflict to change the situational dynamic. In most cases, the third person's involvement is used to strengthen the argument of one particular side and provide enough backing to prove they are right. There are always "sides" in triangulation, and the third person stands in favor of the selfish individual, making them appear smarter, more rational, and morally sound. Since the victim has no backing, they are made to feel like their ideas or arguments are baseless.

Examples of triangulation include bringing a friend or family member into an argument to distract from the real issues, calling an outside party and asking for their opinion to support one person's argument, or making the third person the "judge" who provides the final verdict (often in favor of one person and never equal).

Triangulation can look like

- making the third person feel like their opinion is equally as important in the relationship.
- sharing personal information with a third person makes one partner look bad and the other partner looks good.
- refusing to resolve a conflict without a third person weighing in.

- being shamed and humiliated for not having the support of the third person or being made to feel like your opinions are not valid because they are not supported.

Projection

Projection is the act of imposing your fears, desires, beliefs, and judgments on another person as a way to avoid dealing with how you feel. This is a common tactic used by a narcissist to avoid accountability for their behaviors. It can also be a way of gaslighting the victim and making them believe they are the one who is malicious and manipulative.

Another reason why a narcissist would use projection is to make their partner fear or to be reluctant to advocate for themselves. For example, when the partner attempts to express their needs and set boundaries, the narcissist might say to them, "You only think of yourself." In reality, it is the narcissist who only thinks of themselves, not their partner. However, the more times this belief is projected, the more it is believed to be true.

The projection can look like

- being accused of something that you didn't do.
- being labeled as something that you are not.
- being expected to live up to unrealistic standards.
- having your physical appearance criticized or compared to others.
- being made to feel guilty or responsible for actions that were not your fault.

Generalizations

Generalization refers to making conclusions about an event or situation based on past experiences. In relationships, generalization can be expressed as making sweeping statements about your partner based on general beliefs about a demographic of people. For example, a narcissistic partner might justify their fears of their significant other cheating by saying, "All men/women cheat." Or they might justify their lack of trust in their partner by referring to past experiences of being manipulated by their ex-lovers.

The purpose of using this tactic is to get the victim to believe false ideas about themselves and adjust their behaviors to make the narcissist happy. For example, since nobody wants to be perceived as a cheater, the victim might change the dynamics of their friendships and work relationships to make their narcissistic partner feel comfortable.

Generalizations are another form of subtle guilt-tripping. It is intended to make the victim feel bad for the attitudes and behaviors of other people. Over time, it is common for victims to lose touch with who they are and become a caricature of everything the narcissist believes about them. For example, if the male narcissist believes that women aren't fit to hold corporate jobs, their female partner may adopt this belief and develop a negative perception of working in a corporation.

Generalization can sound like

- "I don't trust men/women."
- "People are only with me for what I can provide."
- "Women are gold diggers."
- "Men are cheaters."

- "Monogamy is a social construct."

Moving the Goalposts

Moving the goalposts is a common tactic used by a narcissist to ensure their partner never succeeds at pleasing them. This is done by unexpectedly changing the rules or standards in the relationship or expressing different needs. Because a narcissist requires an endless amount of validation, they must continuously make their partner work hard at serving them. Therefore, even if their partner is doing an outstanding job at responding to their needs and making them happy, they will expect more instead of showing appreciation for their efforts.

People with codependency issues or perfectionism and people-pleasing tendencies are likely to fall into the trap of going above and beyond to please their narcissistic partners. Due to their feelings of not being good enough, they tend to believe the narcissist when they express being displeased and wanting more. This creates an ongoing cycle of doing the best they can and being disappointed with themselves for not doing enough.

Moving the goalposts can look like

- requesting that you spend more time at home but finding faults with your choice of getting a remote job.
- requesting that you help out with household chores but not being happy with your execution or scheduling.
- encouraging you to start working out but accusing you of spending too much time at the gym.

Love Bombing

Love bombing is a tactic typically used during the idealization or honeymoon stage of a relationship. It is part of the narcissist's strategy to disarm and build a good rapport with the victim. The aim is to make them believe that the affection shown is a sign of legitimate feelings of love.

What makes love bombing manipulative is that the narcissist preys on their partner's desire to be cherished. As a result, they create an illusion of true love to increase their partner's commitment to the relationship. After a short while, the narcissist will withdraw their affection and stop doing the things that led to the build-up of intimacy. However, by this stage, the illusion has been instilled in their partner's minds, and they are willing to hold on to the idea of being loved by the narcissist rather than taking their actions at face value.

Love bombing can look like

- the desire to know everything about you within a few weeks of knowing each other.
- being showered with extravagant gifts without asking for them.
- spending a lot of time together without enough time apart.
- dumping stories of a traumatic childhood to gain sympathy and create an illusion of building trust.
- the pressure to make a commitment and take the relationship further.

Playing on Insecurities

What sometimes passes as "mean behavior" can be a form of psychological manipulation. For instance, when a narcissist is ready to proceed to the devaluation stage, they will use their partner's insecurities against them. In most cases, this is done indirectly to not make the insults seem obvious. For example, if a narcissist knows their partner struggles with body issues, they can play on their insecurities by commenting on their food portions. On the surface, this might seem like a harmless statement or question, but it is emotionally triggering.

Alternatively, a narcissist may change their opinion about their partner's insecurities and go from being supportive and validating to being nasty and judgmental. For example, they might criticize their partner's choice of style, appearance, work ethic, friendships, or hobbies. This is done to make them feel ashamed for being insecure or living a particular lifestyle.

Narcissists know that insecure people believe in their own self-limiting beliefs. Thus, when they are challenged about their insecurities, they are unlikely to stand up for themselves. Instead, they might develop a deeper sense of personal inadequacy and become highly critical of themselves.

Playing on insecurities can look like

- making you feel ashamed for growing up in a certain environment.
- making unkind comments about your physical appearance.
- questioning your work, health, finance, and relationship choices.
- making sweeping generalizations that trigger your insecurities.
- making humiliating comments at your expense and disguising it as humor.

Silent Treatment

Another passive-aggressive manipulation tactic used by narcissists is the silent treatment. This is when one person deliberately ignores or seems unavailable to another person. The aim is to make the person being ignored feel rejected or dismissed and thereby not worthy of attention and validation.

A narcissist needs to feel in control and superior to their significant other at all times. One of the ways to gain more control in an argument or situation is for them to go silent without explaining. Saying nothing creates confusion, frustration, and possibly doubts in the other person's mind and can also make them feel desperate. The silent treatment allows a narcissist to feel more important and dignified than their partner.

Alternatively, the silent treatment can be used as a tactic to punish the victim for actions that may or may not be their fault. Instead of hashing out differences, silence is used to make the victim overthink and feel anxious about what they might have done. This is a form of torture that can send empathetic people into a state of emotional distress and be more willing to do whatever the narcissist says to bring harmony to the relationship.

Silent treatment can look like

- blatantly ignoring you when they can hear you speaking.
- going silent for an extended period without knowing why they are upset or when the silence will end.
- acting distracted when you start to bring up your thoughts and feelings.
- talking to other people but avoiding eye contact and direct communication with you.

Dismissive or Diminishing Comments

During the devaluation and rejection stage of the relationship, a narcissist treats their partner poorly. One of the ways they do this is by dismissing or diminishing their beliefs, thoughts, or contributions. The goal is to make their partner feel inferior and worthless, as though their outlook on life or existence doesn't matter.

Dismissive or diminishing comments invalidate what is being said. For instance, when the victim shares their opinion, the narcissist may respond with an insult, cut them off, or make the opinion seem false or intellectually unsound. Another example is when the victim achieves a remarkable goal, the narcissist might downplay their success and make it seem like nothing significant to celebrate.

Depending on the type of narcissist, dismissive or diminishing comments may be said in public among other people or in private where nobody else can hear. The comments are often based on things the narcissist knows that the victim is insecure about, which makes their comments even more hurtful.

Dismissive or diminishing comments can sound like

- "Don't pretend like you are smart."
- "You can't comment on this topic."
- "You always complain about useless things."
- "You don't know the value of money."
- "You shouldn't wear that color; it doesn't look good on you."

Using Threats or Coercion

Sometimes, psychological manipulation can be aggressive and take on a bullying nature. For instance, if the victim does not do what the narcissist wants them to do, they may use threats, blackmail, or physical violence to force them to do it. These are scare tactics to intimidate the victim and make them less likely to question rules or commands.

Depending on the type of narcissist and their history with violence, the threats could be real or fake. For example, a narcissist may threaten to leave the relationship, and they may or may not follow up with it. Someone else may threaten to inflict self-harm, and they may or may not follow up with it. Regardless of whether the threats are real or fake, most victims treat them as real and will change their behaviors accordingly.

Threats or coercion can sound like

- "If you go out with your friends, you will regret it later."
- "Don't make me angry, or else..."
- "If you leave me, I will hurt myself."
- "I will financially cut you off if you don't listen to me."

It is worth emphasizing that emotional, verbal, or physical abuse of any kind is not acceptable in relationships. If these tactics are ever used to coerce you into taking certain actions, please consider contacting a domestic violence center or hotline and seeking help immediately. If you are based in the US, contact the National Domestic Violence Hotline at 1.800.799.SAFE (7233) or text "START" to 88788.

Part 2

RESPOND

Develop a Strong Defense Against Narcissistic
Abuse by Learning Assertive Communication
and Behavioral Tools

Chapter 5

Safety First—Taking Precautions Before Making Any Decision

How starved you must have been that my heart became a meal for your ego.

–AMANDA TORRONI

Should You Leave?

In the first part of the book, we addressed the first "R" of breaking free from narcissistic abuse, which is "Recognize." We unpacked the definition of narcissism, analyzed the psychology behind narcissistic abuse, and looked at the different faces of narcissism and how narcissistic individuals approach romantic relationships.

We have now reached the second part of the book where we will address the second "R" of breaking free from narcissistic abuse, which is "Respond." Here, we will look at various actions you can take once you have identified signs of narcissism in your romantic relationship.

Victims respond differently when they recognize narcissistic abuse in their relationships. Some might be thankful to learn that what they have been sensing is true but continue to stay in the relationship anyway. Others may be thankful to learn the dark side of their partner and decide to plan their exit strategy from the relationship. There is no right or wrong way to address narcissistic abuse because, ultimately, the decision is solely yours to make. Nevertheless, there are two things to consider when deciding whether to leave or stay.

The first thing to consider is that you cannot change your narcissistic partner. Exposing their behaviors, pleading with them, or trying to fix the power imbalance won't change their motives. They will continue to go through the abuse cycle and ensure their needs are met. Furthermore, since narcissists love competition, putting up resistance could only encourage them to behave more aggressively.

The only time a narcissist changes their behaviors is when they are ready to, and who knows when that will be?

The second thing to consider is the difference between a toxic and abusive relationship. It is common for victims of narcissistic abuse to confuse the two terms and end up downplaying their experience. A toxic relationship refers to a relationship with an unhealthy dynamic. One or both people could have habits that can be described as selfish, manipulative, or disrespectful. Being in a toxic relationship can be draining and lead to unfulfilled needs.

An abusive relationship is the extreme version of a toxic relationship whereby one or both people behave in ways that cause mental, emotional, or physical harm to each other. An abusive relationship doesn't get better with time; it only gets worse. Therefore, the moment behavior becomes abusive and compromises the health and safety of the people in the relationship, it is critical for the couple to separate.

Signs of an Abusive Romantic Relationship

As mentioned earlier, not every individual who displays signs of NPD is necessarily abusive. Nonetheless, they may exhibit behavior that is difficult, inflexible, and self-serving. This also means that you can be in a romantic relationship with a narcissist who is not abusive. *But how can you tell the difference?*

Here are common signs that you are in an abusive relationship. Remember to also check in with your body so you can intuitively sense when your relationship has become abusive.

You Don't Feel Safe

Physical and psychological safety are necessary to regulate your nervous system and make you feel comfortable being close to someone. When you no longer feel safe to either share a space with your partner or share your thoughts and feelings, this is a clear sign there is abuse taking place in the relationship.

You Have Poor or No Communication

Communication is an essential tool to express needs, resolve conflict, and maintain intimacy in a romantic relationship. When there is a lack of communication or none at all, the relationship comes to a standstill. This may lead to trust issues and make it difficult to hold each other accountable for making the relationship work. Communicating about problems can also be a sign of your partner's willingness to change. If they avoid doing this, there is no evidence of their willingness to change.

You Feel Exploited

It is normal for relationships to have an imbalance of give-and-take. For example, during some periods, you and your partner may take turns investing more time and effort into performing positive habits and doing what it takes to keep the relationship going. However, when it is only you who is trying to make the relationship work by adjusting your behaviors or making an effort to respond to your partner's needs, this could be a sign of extreme dysfunction.

You Lose Touch With Who You Are

Abusers tend to psychologically break down their victims to the extent of them disconnecting from their reality. This is done through various manipulation tactics like gaslighting, projection, or playing on insecurities. When you start to question your beliefs or identity or find yourself behaving in ways that don't align with who you are, take a moment to pause and check in with yourself. An abusive partner will never accept you as you are and may demand that you change to receive their approval.

You Feel Belittled or Shamed

Healthy relationships are built on respect, reciprocity, and acceptance. When you start feeling like you are walking on eggshells or must adjust your behaviors in the presence of your partner, you may very well be in an emotionally abusive relationship. Abusers use shame to diminish their victims and slowly chip away at their sense of self-worth. They do this long enough until their victims internalize the shame and launch an attack on their own identity. Weaponizing shame is a destructive manipulation tactic that can lead to mental health problems like suicidal thinking and depression.

If you have recognized the signs of abuse in your relationship and are ready to walk away, you have the right to do so. Choosing yourself in this type of situation is not selfish but rather an act of self-love. However, before you can get up and leave, there are a few precautions to take to make a safe exit.

The Importance of Safety When Leaving an Abuser

A narcissist invests a lot of time to make sure you can't leave them. Remember, even if they don't show any signs of love anymore, they need to keep you as a source of narcissistic supply. The constant psychological manipulation (and, in some relationships, domestic violence) is supposed to make it harder for you to walk out of the relationship.

Therefore, when you decide to leave, it is crucial to spend time thinking about how you are going to leave safely. You have probably seen your partner have explosive anger episodes after minor incidents, now imagine how angry they will be when you announce that you are leaving. Additionally, having discussions about leaving with a manipulative and apathetic individual may work against you. They already know what to say to trigger certain emotions and either make you scared of leaving them or hopeful that things will get better in your relationship.

Safety planning is critical leading up to you leaving the relationship. It enables you to do research and think strategically about how you are going to leave as well as the best ways to protect yourself in the process. When you create a safety plan, you are encouraged to think about every possible scenario and determine what actions you will take to cope under those conditions. Moreover, you can think about and devise a plan on ways to seek community support from friends, family, and coworkers.

A good safety plan will have the following key elements:

- essential items to pack and leave with
- safety precautions to take at home before and on the day
- a plan on how you will protect and involve your children
- the role of neighbors and work colleagues in keeping you safe

In the following sections, we will discuss each element as well as practical steps and checklists to follow.

Essential Items to Pack and Leave With

A few days or weeks before you leave, start collecting and putting aside important documents that you are going to need. Once you drive out of the driveway, the aim is to never return to the house or apartment where you reside with your partner, unless you are accompanied by someone else. Therefore, it is important to take as much as you can fit into your vehicle, placing more priority on the following list of items.

Essential Items	Yes/No
Legal documents (e.g. passport, ID document, business registration certificates, marriage certificate, immigration papers, driver's license, school records, bank account information)	
Money (e.g. bank cards, emergency cash, checkbooks)	
Security (e.g. keys to your house, workplace, car, safety deposit box)	
Technological devices (e.g. cell phones, laptops, tablets, chargers)	
Health (e.g. health cards, medication, prescriptions, medical equipment)	
Suitcase of clothing for each individual	

Safety Precautions to Take at Home Before and on the Day

Once you have checked off the essential items, the next step is to create your emergency safety plan. The plan starts a few hours or days before you leave and includes all of the action steps you will need to take to leave your home safely. Below are examples of two emergency safety plans: one for when you are living with your partner and another one for when you live in separate properties.

A safety plan when you are living with your partner:

Emergency Safety Plan	Yes/No
Gather your essential items in one place or plan where you will find them and quickly grab them.	
Create a list of emergency contact numbers including friends, family, local police station, and local support groups and shelters.	
Make arrangements with a close friend or family member who you trust to stay with for a certain length of time.	
Study what triggers your partner's rage or episodes so you can predict the next incident and identify the best time to leave.	

Emergency Safety Plan	Yes/No
Check your car for a GPS device that your partner may have installed to track your movements. Inspect your car every day to easily pick up on changes that are out of the ordinary. Also, make sure you turn off any tracking apps on your phone when you leave.	
Teach your children how to call the police or family members when they are in trouble (you can also create a safety plan for your children).	
Be aware of any weapons your partner may have hidden in the house.	
Clear the cache and history files on your home computer before the day you leave (it is recommended to do research on a public computer at a library or internet cafe instead of using your home computer).	

A safety plan when you are living in separate properties:

Emergency Safety Plan	Yes/No
Provide close friends or family with a script of what to tell your partner when they cannot reach you on the phone.	
Change the keys and locks to your house and install a new alarm system.	
Install a motion detection lighting system outside of your house to alert you when somebody is within a certain distance from your points of entry and exit.	
Check whether you are eligible for a protective order under your state and jurisdiction.	
Replace your current doors, windows, and garage with automatic self-locking systems.	
Change the passwords on your email, apps, and websites.	
Check your car for a GPS device that your partner may have installed to track your movements. Inspect your car every day to easily pick up on changes that are out of the ordinary.	

Emergency Safety Plan	Yes/No
If possible, change the model and make of your car or use e-hailing services to get you from point A to point B during the first few months.	
Record all phone calls (where legal) and document communication made via email or text with your partner.	

How to Protect and Involve Your Children

If you have children who are living at home, it is important to include them as part of your safety planning. For instance, depending on their age, they may need to be aware that in a few days, they are going to leave the home because of the unhealthy environment. You may also need to empower them with self-defense skills, such as learning how to detect a threatening situation, call the police, or protect themselves in violent situations.

Here are a few more tips for protecting and involving your children:

- Teach your children how to set and disarm the alarm system.
- Create a safe room that leads to an exit out of the house.
- Emphasize the point that in a hostile situation at home, their safety is the priority and they should focus on getting themselves in a safe place.
- Create a code word or sign to use with your children when they need to call for help or run to safety.

- Run through the process of calling for help and identify the different people they should call in specific situations.
- Ensure that your young children know the residential addresses and contact numbers of emergency contact people by heart.
- Rehearse what your child can say on the phone when asking for help.

The Role of Neighbors and Work Colleagues in Keeping You Safe

Depending on the level of community involvement you want when planning to leave an abusive relationship, you can reach out to neighbors and work colleagues whom you know and trust and provide instructions on how they can protect you over the first few months of walking out of your relationship.

Here is an example of ways to involve neighbors in your safety planning:

- Notify your neighbors of when they should call the police, such as when they notice suspicious activity or hear yelling and screaming.
- Create a code word or sign to use with your children when they need to call for help.
- If you live separately from your partner, notify neighbors that they no longer live with you and should call you immediately when they see their car in the neighborhood or see them near your home.
- Arrange with one of your neighbors to take care of your children during an emergency.

Here is an example of ways to involve work colleagues in your safety planning:

- Show your work colleagues and security guards a picture of your partner and describe their car to make them aware of what they look like.
- Ask your work colleagues to avoid sharing any personal information about your whereabouts or current living arrangements.
- Ask your manager or the IT department to have your calls screened. Document any unwarranted calls from your partner.
- Have a security guard walk you to your car at the end of your work day.
- Discuss the possibility of coming to work earlier and leaving earlier to switch up your commute times during the first few months.
- If possible, ask to work from home for the first few weeks or months until your situation stabilizes.

Practice Self-Care After Breaking Free From Narcissistic Abuse

What happens after you leave an abusive relationship? Do you start to live your life as normal?

For the most part, your weekday routines, which include going to work and picking up your children from school, will stay the same. However, your weekends will be dedicated to self-care!

Self-care can be defined as being responsive to your physical, mental, and emotional needs. It requires you to be in tune with your mind and body and listen to the cues you are being given. If your body needs rest, getting to bed early would be a form of self-care. When you are emotional but can't figure out why, journaling or spending time outside would be considered a form of self-care.

The reason why self-care is critical in the weeks and months after leaving a narcissistic abusive relationship is because you have a backlog of needs to attend to. For so long, you have prioritized your partner's needs and denied your own, and now you can solely focus on things that make you feel balanced, content, and fulfilled.

Self-care is also a type of self-healing where you explore and process your pain and cry as much as you like if that is what you need. Perhaps you are still confused about what was real or imagined about your relationship or have a lot of internalized anger to release. Practicing self-care can help you acknowledge the impact of being in a narcissistic abusive relationship and take the necessary steps to heal.

Here are five immediate self-care practices to carry out on the days, weeks, and months following your break up.

Practice No Contact

Your narcissistic ex-partner, who is manipulative by nature, will attempt to reach out to you and convince you to take them back. If they can reach you on the phone, they will make false promises, go through another round of love bombing, pretend to be remorseful, or use threats to force you to go back. The more talking that occurs between you, the easier it is for them to get inside of your mind again. It is, therefore, better to avoid contact with them altogether or limit the contact if you have joint custody of your children (i.e., only call or text regarding the welfare of your children).

Acknowledge the Abuse

Now that you have some time to reflect on your relationship, help yourself get to a place where you can acknowledge that you were in an abusive relationship. This doesn't mean that you should forget the good times; however, these were only few and far between. Read books or attend support groups for survivors of narcissistic abuse so that you can come to accept the harmful psychological manipulation that you were subjected to. The purpose of this exercise is not to find reasons to resent your ex-partner but, instead, to start the healing process and address the psychological damage already done.

Resist the Urge to Blame Yourself

Narcissists train their victims to feel responsible for the conflict and dysfunction of the relationship. Now that you are free from the manipulation, it is important to resist the urge to blame yourself for walking away. While you are not perfect and probably have some work to do, it is unfair to blame yourself for the abuse experienced in your relationship or for not doing anything sooner. It takes a really brave person to identify and respond to narcissistic abuse, so give yourself credit for going through the process to end the abusive cycle.

Focus on Healing Your Inner Wounds

Begin the process of healing your inner wounds by connecting the dots between your earliest childhood experiences and the patterns in your adult relationships. Travel as far back as your earliest memories of your relationship with your parents and identify behaviors that occurred then that have shaped the type of people you are attracted to, your fear of setting boundaries or expressing your needs, or your need for validation in romantic relationships. Seeking professional counseling can be a great decision to take at this point so you can receive expert guidance on how to let go of limiting beliefs, heal trauma, and learn the tools to form healthy relationships.

Spend Time Rediscovering Yourself

Self-care should be about prioritizing your well-being and reconnecting to who you were before you met your narcissistic ex-partner. Rediscovering yourself describes the process of learning more about your personality strengths and weaknesses, passions and interests, goals and ambitions, and your values and beliefs. This is a time to explore beyond your comfort zone and try out new experiences that can help you strengthen your self-concept. Have fun reinventing your self-image, picking up new hobbies, and meeting cool and interesting people!

Chapter 6

Deal With Facts, Not Feelings

But that's the thing about narcissists. They can try to fool you, with all their heart, but in the end, they're just fooling themselves.

– ELLIE FOX

Why Narcissists Avoid the Truth

If leaving your romantic relationship is not a decision you are willing to make right now, then you will need to learn a few communication and behavioral tools to help you avoid attempts at manipulation. However, you should be warned: Narcissists are masters at deception, so you will need to practice these tools regularly to build a strong defense. Furthermore, the communication and behavioral tools offered in this book do not replace seeking professional counseling.

To protect yourself against psychological manipulation, you will need to recognize a few things about your narcissistic partner. The first is that they know you better than you think. Your partner has taken the time to study your behaviors, test your boundaries, and learn your triggers. They know how to push your buttons by saying certain words or carrying out certain behaviors.

To prevent them from spinning lies and creating drama, you will need to spend time getting to know yourself and deepening your self-awareness. Through practices like meditation and journaling, explore your strengths and weaknesses, uncover childhood pain, and learn more about the emotional issues that make you vulnerable to manipulation, such as being a people-pleaser or having a deep-seated abandonment wound.

The second thing to recognize about your partner is they purposefully avoid being called out for their behaviors. Narcissists run away from the truth about who they are so that they don't have to apologize or take accountability for their actions. In their fantasy world, they are always right and others are always wrong. Even when you show them how their actions have negatively impacted you, they will deny, downplay, or diminish what you are saying.

There is a psychological explanation for why narcissists avoid the truth. Doctors have found that people diagnosed with NPD lack whole object relations (WOR). WOR is the ability to see objects in a balanced way, as having positive *and* negative qualities. For narcissists who lack this, they see relationships and things as either positive or negative but not both. Narcissists see themselves and other people as being good or bad. They build their self-image on the belief of being good and having good intentions for why they take certain actions. This all-positive self-image is what justifies their sense of entitlement and superiority complex.

Since they perceive themselves as being good, they find ways to convince others that their decisions cannot be bad. When they are caught telling a lie, cheating, or manipulating their partners, they find reasons to prove that their motives were good. For example, a narcissistic individual who tells their partner they are overweight and unattractive may tell themselves they are being supportive. Another narcissistic individual who cheats on their partner might find a way to prove that their infidelity was done in the best interests of the relationship.

Furthermore, the fact that narcissists choose to believe only the good about themselves means they are likely to shut down or project their feelings when they are confronted about their actions. These factors are what makes building a strong psychological defense challenging. But the good news is that the more you practice these communication and behavioral tools, the better you will get at holding your own in the relationship!

Learn How to Mask Your Vulnerability

One of the worst-kept secrets of a narcissist is that they are extremely sensitive to criticism. Whenever they are corrected, given feedback, or confronted about their actions, they tend to feel diminished and disrespected. Think back to a time when you attempted to express your needs to your partner and an argument suddenly erupted. This happens because your partner generally has a hard time being shown their faults and accepting responsibility for their actions.

Due to unresolved childhood trauma, your partner's emotional maturity has been stunted and this causes them to accept feedback the same way a child would throw a tantrum for being told no. To compensate for feeling criticized by you, they may launch a vile attack on your character and use all types of psychological tricks to make you regret pointing out their weaknesses.

Whenever you are faced with this kind of situation, recognize what is happening. Play back how the situation unfolded and how your partner has chosen to react. Remind yourself that your partner has severe insecurities that make it difficult for them to listen to any constructive feedback.

As the vile attacks continue, maintain a straight face and avoid showing your partner that you are affected by their attempts to pull you down. Remember that they have studied you and are aware of what words or actions trigger your insecurities. Since they are feeling attacked, they will retaliate by targeting your vulnerabilities. Recognize their strategy and continue to seem unbothered. Do not react to their words or behaviors like you normally would.

Seeing that their default moves aren't working, your partner may employ other manipulation tactics like playing the victim card or bringing up mistakes you have made in the past. Continue to keep a straight face and mask your vulnerabilities. Preferably, do not respond while these attacks are taking place. Simply look at them and focus on taking deep breaths. If they bait you into saying something, respond with "I will wait until you are finished talking and then I will speak." Your partner could be relentless in finding ways to hurt your feelings but don't show any signs of their tactics working.

Here are a few more strategies you can practice to mask your vulnerabilities and remain unbreakable during psychological attacks.

Avoid Stooping to Their Level

When you are being provoked, there is a natural urge to defend yourself. You might be tempted to throw back violent insults to hurt your partner and level the score. However, this is all a part of their trick to fuel the conflict and mentally and emotionally exhaust you. By all means, avoid playing the narcissist's game by stooping low. This will render them powerless to break you down. Your silence will speak volumes about your intolerance for aggressive behavior.

Stick to the Facts

Direct the conversation toward the facts of the situation. Unlike emotions, facts are reliable, unbiased, and based on reality. It is difficult to dispute facts when they are evident for both of you to see. Whenever your partner tries to make emotional appeals or insists that you consider how they are emotionally impacted, validate how they may be feeling and shift the conversation back to the facts.

You might say, "I hear that you are upset, but we have gone off topic and I would like us to speak about the incident that took place earlier." If your partner tends to distort the truth, keep a record of conversations, receipts, emails, videos, and images of your interactions with them and other people to provide factual evidence.

Don't Seek Their Approval

Since narcissists often move the goalposts, it is pointless trying to win their approval. Your partner will never make you feel like you are doing enough to make them happy. There will always be more that you could've done. Seeking your partner's approval can also trigger feelings of inadequacy or rejection wounds. If your partner knows this, they will deliberately invalidate you. It is, therefore, important to practice validating yourself by acknowledging the effort you are making to be a good partner.

When your partner tries to make you feel guilty for not doing enough, remind yourself that you are two separate individuals with two separate outlooks on the world. Their opinions are not higher or more credible than yours. They are simply *their* opinions. Choose to validate your own beliefs and opinions. For instance, if you genuinely believe you did a good job, hold on to that belief and pat yourself on the back!

Don't Take the Slander Personally

Narcissists have no filter. They say whatever they need to say to achieve their aims. Many times, they do not think before they speak and later won't regret the hurtful comments they make. When dealing with such a person, don't take what they say to heart. Their comments are not a true reflection of reality nor are they a true reflection of who you are. Repeatedly ask yourself this question: *How can I trust the words of someone who is intentionally trying to hurt me?* The truth is you cannot because what they say has a dark agenda behind it.

Communicate With Power and Assertiveness

You have managed to keep calm and collected during your partner's fit of rage, but now it is time for you to speak. *What are you going to say?*

Communication with a narcissist doesn't sound the same as communication with another close friend or family member. Due to their manipulative nature, you cannot be as open and vulnerable as you would be when talking with other close people. Everything you say must be factual instead of emotional and get straight to the point. In essence, the goal is to provide few loopholes for them to hook their claws into your message and twist your words.

Something else worth considering is your nonverbal body language. When speaking to your partner, never appear weak or intimidated by them. Stand up tall, maintain eye contact, and mask your vulnerability. Clear your throat before you start talking and take a deep breath. Mentally repeat this mantra to yourself: *I am capable. I am strong. I am in control.*

If you are intimidated by the facial expressions or body language of your partner, remind yourself about their worst-kept secret: They are plagued with insecurities and compensate for their inferiority complex by appearing strong. Therefore, rest assured that both of you feel equally nervous about how the conversation is going to go. Your advantage, however, is that you have a toolbox of powerful communication tools to outsmart your partner.

Consider the following communication tools tailored to combat common narcissistic tendencies.

Paraphrase What You Hear Being Said

Narcissists do not like to use logic when making arguments because that would quickly catch them out. They prefer to speak in riddles and metaphors or contradict themselves to confuse. To ensure that your conversations are productive and real issues can be addressed, paraphrase what your partner is saying and repeat it back to them. Give them a chance to either agree or disagree with how you have understood them, then share your opinion.

Here is an example of what you might say:

"It is important for me to fully understand what you are saying. Correct me if I'm wrong, but are you saying that you feel that I haven't given you enough attention since we had our first child?"

Use the PCC Method

PCC stands for praise, confront, and compliment (Up Journey, 2021). This technique helps you express thoughts and feelings that may be difficult for your partner to hear without wounding their ego. While you have the right to speak your mind, consider the fact that your partner is extremely sensitive to anything that may sound close to rejection. When using this technique, start by offering praise, then being clear and specific about your stance on the issue at hand, and end off by finding one thing to compliment your partner on.

Here is an example of how you might use the PCC method:

"I appreciate you for sitting down with me to have this chat. The reason I wanted us to meet is to address the lack of reciprocation in our relationship. At the beginning of our relationship, you did an amazing job of being responsive to my needs. Now, I feel like you don't notice when I am sad. I miss that connection and would like us to discuss how to go back there because I think you can be a great partner."

Have a Clear Objective for Conversations

Before sitting down with your partner, write down a clear objective for the conversation and a few points you would like to make. If the conversation is impromptu, take a few minutes to think about the core message you want to bring across to your partner. Having an objective for your conversations helps you stay on track and have meaningful exchanges. Moreover, your partner will have a difficult time dodging and ducking from addressing the core issue at hand. Another way to stay on track is to keep your conversations short and give each other time to reflect on what was shared.

Here is an example of communicating clear objectives:

"We need to speak about my parents coming over this weekend. I would like for us to focus on the specific plans we have for them and avoid bringing up the tension between you and my father."

Maintain a Neutral Stance

Part of a narcissist's agenda is to get you to reject your viewpoint and accept their viewpoint. For example, while expressing your hurt feelings, your partner might look for errors in your thinking or project their feelings onto you to make you second-guess yourself. You shouldn't immediately abandon your ideas just because someone else doesn't agree with them nor should you enter a debate about semantics or perceptions. This will only lead you back to being emotional, which creates room for your partner to pull you down.

If you have been shown your faults, the best option is to maintain a neutral stance. Do not agree or disagree with your partner. Your response should be short and dull to not give them enough ammunition to use against you.

Here is an example of how you might maintain a neutral stance:

"Thank you for sharing your opinion, however, that's not how I see things. With that said, let's shift our focus back to the main issue at hand."

Signs You Should Walk Away From a Conversation

You should not underestimate the psychological damage that can be caused by one conversation that goes too far. Certain words or behaviors spoken by your partner can leave a deep emotional wound that requires more than an apology to heal.

When speaking to someone who believes they are above rules and lacks empathy, your safety is extremely important. There will be times during a conversation with your partner when your gut instinct will kick in and you will feel unsafe or fearful. That is usually the point at which you must walk away regardless of how much progress you have made in the conversation.

Here are clear signs that the conversation has become unproductive and should be ended:

- You are finding it difficult to remain rational and keep a straight face.
- You feel physical signs that you are losing control of yourself, such as an increased heart rate, sweating, stuttering, or becoming tearful.
- Your partner is gradually escalating their voice and using aggressive body language to rile themselves up.
- The boundaries you had set at the beginning of the conversation (e.g., not interrupting while someone else is speaking) have been violated several times.
- You can sense that if the conversation continues for a few more minutes, one of you will break out of character.

How you conduct yourself around a narcissist should always be calm and dignified, even when you are choosing to walk away from a conversation. This ensures that whatever thoughts or emotions they are projecting onto you don't land the way they would hope.

Below are five calm and dignified steps to practice when walking away from an unsafe and unproductive conversation with your partner.

Step 1: Describe What You Are Noticing

Describe the behavior you are noticing that has made you feel unsafe and unwilling to continue the conversation. Use "I" statements to make it about you. For example, you might say "I am noticing that you speak over me and won't allow me to finish my thoughts." If possible, make these statements as objective and factual as possible.

Do not attack their personality or make accusations about their motives.

Step 2: Describe the Impact of What You Are Noticing

Follow up by describing how their behavior threatens the quality of the conversation. Once again, logic is better than emotions when speaking to a narcissist. For example, instead of saying, "You know how much I hate it when you speak over me," you could say, "If you don't give me a chance to respond to you, this cannot be a constructive conversation."

Step 3: State the Need for a Break

Present a way forward by stating the need for a break and explaining how this can lead to a more constructive conversation later. Be assertive in stating what needs to happen instead of asking for permission. In essence, by stating that you need a break, you are creating a boundary and setting a precedence for future conversations. A simple statement you can use is: "The best thing to do is for us to take a break and resume this discussion later."

Step 4: Let Your Partner Know When You Will Reengage With Them and How

Do not leave your partner guessing about the next time this conversation will be brought up. State how much time you need and when you will be ready to reengage. Moreover, specify under which circumstances you would be willing to speak with them again. For example, you might expect them to be in a calm mood and adhere to the conversation boundaries you set. You might say, "I need the rest of the weekend to reflect on this issue. I am open to reengaging with you sometime next week. However, I need you to respect my boundaries or else we will have to end the conversation again."

Step 5: Get Up and Walk Away

The final step is to physically get up and leave the area or room. No further communication can take place for at least 30 minutes. Tensions may be running high and both you and your partner need some time alone. If they attempt to bring up the same topic of conversation before the agreed-upon time, disengage immediately and walk away. Say something like, "I told you that I need a weekend to reflect. Please respect my wishes."

Chapter 7

Break Free From Codependency

Many of us live in denial of who we truly are because we fear losing someone or something and there are times that if we don't rock the boat, too often the one we lose is ourselves.

−DENNIS MERRITT JONES

The Narcissism-Codependency Dynamic

To make a relationship work with a narcissistic individual, you must be willing to identify aspects of your personality that make it easy for your partner to manipulate you and find ways to address those issues.

For instance, it is common for people who date or marry narcissists to suffer from codependency issues. Codependency is a behavioral pattern of going above and beyond for others to seek their approval. It stems from early childhood neglect and abandonment by caregivers.

Children who are raised by emotionally unavailable parents grow up to crave the affection they did not receive. At the root of codependency is a need for validation, someone to notice and say, "I am proud of you." Narcissists quickly pick up on this need during the early stages of meeting their new victims and use it as leverage to manipulate them.

Codependency has many different faces and characteristics. However, people who are codependent on others tend to display one or more of the following traits:

- the need to fix or rescue others
- taking on more responsibility than one can bear
- overcommitting and feeling guilty for canceling plans
- the fear of expressing thoughts and feelings openly
- the tendency to side with others on a particular viewpoint
- the need for recognition disguised as offering a helping hand
- feeling responsible for the well-being of others
- the fear of being abandoned by friends and family
- the fear or difficulty accepting change
- internalizing anger to avoid upsetting others

Read over the traits above again and reflect on your romantic relationship patterns. Do you find yourself feeling attracted to people who need you? Do you feel validated whenever you can help someone? And do you struggle to give up on love even when you see the red flags?

If you can identify as someone with codependency issues, you are unconsciously attracted to people with narcissistic tendencies for several reasons. The first and most obvious reason is the fact that narcissists are extremely charming and confident. They have an "I don't care what others think" aura about them that you wish you could channel. Narcissists can be highly intuitive and good at reading between the lines. With just one look into your eyes, they can connect to how you are feeling and describe your emotional experience better than you can.

Being around this larger-than-life personality can make you feel brave and help you overcome some of your insecurities. At the beginning of the relationship, they are capable of making you feel a deep love that you have never felt for anybody else. However, there is a price to pay when being in a relationship with a narcissist, which is to make them the center of your life.

Initially, you are more than happy to pay this price because it affirms a relationship pattern that began as a kid. Living with an inconsistent parent, you learned how to give more than you expect to receive. Over time, you start to see the dark side of a narcissist, the side that resembles pure evil. What they expect from you continues to change and becomes more outrageous. You become worn out at trying to be the best partner you can be and being criticized for your efforts.

Your narcissistic partner triggers your childhood wounds in the worst possible way and you may start to believe that you were never destined to receive unconditional love from others.

Break the Cycle of Codependency

If you identify as someone with codependency issues, you are probably looking for an affectionate and nurturing partner because that is what you were denied as a child. However, how you go about searching for these traits in others is not effective. For example, instead of going for the typical good woman or man who doesn't have any red flags and is open to love, you are excited by the typical toxic woman or man who looks mysterious, plays hard to get, and isn't looking for commitment.

Doesn't this seem like a contradiction? Why would someone who desires affection and nurturing find someone who is emotionally unavailable magnetizing?

The answer is because that is the only pattern you have been modeled from childhood. If you have never seen or felt true compassion and acceptance from your parents or close family, you are not consciously drawn to those traits in others. Instead, you may be drawn to hot-and-cold behavior, where affection is given and withdrawn regularly. Moreover, a romantic relationship without any drama may feel boring and loveless to you, particularly if you grew up in a household where drama was the order of the day.

The good news is that you can break the cycle of codependency and teach yourself how to be open to genuine loving relationships that don't reinforce harmful patterns. The first step is to recognize the stages of codependency.

Early Stage

The early stage of codependency feels like being infatuated with your partner. This is common in new romantic relationships and therefore may not seem to you like an early sign of codependency. Some of the symptoms you may exhibit at this stage include obsessively thinking about your partner, having trouble setting boundaries in your relationship, and making excuses for your partner's questionable behaviors.

If you are in a relationship with a narcissistic individual, the early stage of codependency occurs around the same time as the idealization stage of the narcissistic abuse cycle.

Middle Stage

The middle stage of codependency can feel overwhelming, as this is usually when you start losing control of your tendencies to please your partner. For instance, you may agree to do things that you are uncomfortable with just to make your partner happy or significantly change your routines to allow for more time with your partner. Time apart from your partner or not hearing from them for the whole day may send your body into a state of panic. This happens because, at this stage, you have become enmeshed with your partner and feel physical symptoms of stress when they are not around.

If you are in a relationship with a narcissistic individual, you might enable their manipulative behaviors to maintain harmony in your relationship. It may also be difficult for you to confront them for their problematic behaviors because you fear upsetting them to the point of sabotaging your relationship.

Late Stage

The late stage of codependency occurs when your relationship starts feeling so stressful that you turn to destructive coping mechanisms, such as working, drinking, or eating excessively. Other mental and physical symptoms you may experience include anxiety, depression, fatigue, migraines, and insomnia. What makes this stage of codependency alarming is that the obsessive behavior displayed at the beginning of your relationship intensifies and you may find desperate ways of holding on to the relationship, such as isolating yourself from friends and family, hacking your partner's devices, placing trackers to learn their whereabouts, and completely abandoning yourself to gain your partner's acceptance.

If you are in a relationship with a narcissistic individual, the late stage of codependency often occurs around the same time as the rejection stage of the narcissistic abuse cycle. The more your partner pushes you away, the more desperate you become to bring them near. This push-and-pull dynamic can take a severe toll on your self-esteem and make you vulnerable to depression.

Breaking the cycle of codependency is about recognizing which stage you are currently in and how much of your identity you have lost in your relationship. Since codependency is caused by early childhood experiences, you will also need to travel back into your childhood and reprocess events that may have scarred you. But ultimately, breaking free from codependency is a lifelong journey that begins with self-awareness. If you are interested in learning more about codependency and various strategies to heal from this behavioral pattern, purchase my book titled *The Codependency Healing Workbook: A Comprehensive Guide For Restoring Self-Worth, Breaking Free From Unhealthy Relationships, And Setting Healthy Boundaries (Self-Blossoming Emotions Book 2)* from Amazon today!

Recognize You Have Needs

An issue that is related to codependency is the fear or reluctance to express your needs to your partner. Perhaps you aren't sure what you need or you have an idea but can't find the words to communicate it.

As you can imagine, narcissistic individuals are drawn to people who don't have strong boundaries and, therefore, cannot express their needs. Ideally, they are looking for a "yes" person who won't deny their requests. However, the reality is that even the most agreeable, self-sacrificing person has needs—this is part of what makes us human.

Denying your needs is like saying you can survive without oxygen. Your physical, mental, and emotional needs are what keep you alive and healthy. Of course, your partner is not supposed to respond to every single need. For instance, you are capable of taking care of your basic needs like the need for food, shelter, clothing, and security. However, since you are in an intimate relationship, they can help you respond to your emotional needs, such as the need for love, support, and acceptance.

It may be easier for you to recognize basic survival needs but harder to recognize emotional needs. One of the explanations for this could be that as a child, your emotional needs were ignored, denied, or downplayed by your parents. In your adult romantic relationships, you may fear experiencing rejection for expressing your emotional needs, hence the decision to push them down.

To avoid being exploited in your relationship, it is important to start expressing your emotions. But before you can do that, you must recognize what they are. Consider the following five core emotional needs:

1. The need to feel safe.
2. The need for autonomy, to feel competent, and to express a sense of identity.
3. The need to freely express emotions and desires.
4. The need to be playful and act spontaneously.
5. The need for self-control and being guided to set healthy limits.

Bring out a piece of paper and pen and for each need, write a full page about the various ways your partner can respond to it. For example, describe several ways your partner can make you feel safe. This may include things like helping you manage household finances, reaffirming your love regularly, setting boundaries with friends and family that respect your relationship, and so on.

This exercise may be difficult if you have never had these needs fulfilled in other relationships before. To overcome this barrier, seek to tap into your intuition and sense what each need feels like. For example, you can try to focus meditation and bring the word "safety" to the front of your mind and tune in to the physical sensations or inspired thoughts that come to your mind. Take down notes afterward of what you believe safety to feel or look like.

Communicating your needs to your partner is as simple as using the "I feel/I need" sentence structure. You start by stating what you are feeling as a result of an unmet need. Note that this is an emotional experience taking place inside of you that your partner may not be aware of, so be as clear as possible when explaining how you feel. The second part involves expressing a need that can make you feel better. It is recommended to think for a while about this before approaching your partner so that you can offer a lot of detail and description to help them take action.

Consider the following example:

I feel undermined and humiliated when you make nasty jokes at my expense in front of other people. I need you to show more compassion toward my feelings and consider how you make me look in front of people.

Now it's your turn. Think of a recent scenario where you felt upset with your partner but decided to say nothing about it. Use the "I feel/I need" sentence structure to express your feelings and needs.

Part 3

RECLAIM

Repel Narcissists by Developing a Healthy
Sense of Self-Worth, Setting Boundaries, and
Taking Control of Your Life Narrative

Chapter 8

Communicate and Enforce Boundaries

Those who get angry when you set a boundary are the ones you need to set boundaries for.

–J.S. WOLFE

The Lack of Boundaries in Abusive Relationships

We have covered two "Rs" of breaking free from narcissistic abuse, which are "Recognize" and "Respond." Some of the topics we have explored include defining NPD, describing a list of psychological manipulation tactics narcissistic partners use, and looking at effective communication and behavioral tools to build a strong psychological defense against narcissistic tendencies.

We have now reached the third and final part of the book where we will delve into the third "R" which is "Reclaim." After you have identified narcissistic abuse and responded appropriately by either leaving the relationship or adjusting your behaviors, you are ready to reclaim your power by connecting to your authentic self and regaining a sense of pride and independence.

The only power a narcissistic partner has over you is the power you give to them.

Without your physical, mental, and emotional consent, your partner's manipulation tactics won't work on you. One of the most valuable lessons you can learn on your road to recovery from narcissistic abuse is the ability to draw boundaries without feeling guilt or shame.

Boundaries are the personal limits you set between you and others. In a romantic relationship, they help you determine how much time, energy, money, affection, and attention to give your partner until you cannot give anymore. Moreover, boundaries help you explain what type of behavior you cannot accept from your partner. Thus, having boundaries is the same as enforcing standards in your relationship.

In general, narcissists gravitate toward people with weak or nonexistent boundaries. Weak boundaries are limits that are not communicated clearly or that don't come with consequences. For example, telling your partner you don't like to be cursed at is a boundary, but failing to enforce a consequence when it is violated makes it difficult for your partner to take you seriously.

The reason why your partner dislikes boundaries is that they don't want to be challenged or held accountable for their harmful behaviors. Essentially, they want to get away with hurting you. Remember that narcissists enter romantic relationships to serve their interests. If you stop your partner from getting their needs fulfilled, they will react with rage.

Part of the reason why your partner placed you on a pedestal early on in the relationship was to cause you to become so mesmerized by them that you relax your boundaries or make exceptions. For example, the gifts, attention, and affection were distractions to get you to spend more time with them (if you had a strict routine and schedule) or have sex early on (if you had a rule about waiting a while before being intimate).

During the devaluation and rejection stage of the abuse cycle, your boundaries are tested again. However, this time, you are interrogated, ridiculed, and made to feel silly for enforcing limits. Your partner's objective during these stages is to plant enough seeds of doubt that you willingly adjust or lose your boundaries.

Steps to Reestablish Boundaries

Victims of narcissistic abuse have countless boundary violations, which is evident by the extreme physical and mental health crises they experience after years of being in a relationship with a narcissistic individual. By the time many victims are ready to seek help and break free from narcissistic abuse, they lack a sense of self-worth and cannot even describe their limits.

This does not have to be your experience. You do not have to reach this point.

To reclaim your power and regain control over your mind and body, reestablishing healthy boundaries is essential. Think of your boundaries as your constitution that informs others about who you are and how you would like to be treated. Having boundaries in a romantic relationship is not selfish, rather it is an act of self-love. It teaches you to respect your needs and pay attention to how people and situations make you feel. Moreover, it instills a positive belief that you are worthy of being cared for and honored because that is what you expect from yourself and others.

So, how do you reestablish your boundaries? Follow these simple steps.

Step 1: Get Familiar With Different Types of Boundaries

Your romantic relationship has a unique dynamic and culture. How you and your partner relate with each other is different from how you relate with your best friends or work colleagues. As a result, the boundaries you establish must be relevant to the needs and everyday interactions of your relationship.

There are different types of boundaries that you can enforce to feel safe and supported in your relationship. A few of them include

- personal space
- finances
- household chores
- communication
- intimacy
- quality time
- privacy and security
- use of social media and devices

When deciding on what type of boundaries you need, reflect on the areas where you feel most stressed or frustrated in your relationship. For example, do you often complain about the household chores because you feel that you aren't being assisted enough? Or do you feel anxious whenever you need to share your feelings with your partner because they are not a good communicator? Make these areas of your relationship a priority when deciding on the type of boundaries to establish.

Step 2: Write Down Your Preferences

At this stage, you should have a general idea of what type of boundary you are going to establish and why this is important for you. The next step is to write down the preferred actions and behaviors you would like your partner to take. For example, if time is one of your boundaries, you can describe what standards you would like your partner to uphold regarding spending quality time with you.

Stick to a maximum of two preferences for each boundary and make your requests simple and easy to follow. If you are setting a boundary around quality time, your preferences could be to

- spend time together with the TV switched off on weeknights.
- eat breakfast together in the mornings.

Preferences are "nice to have" negotiable boundaries. This means that your partner is allowed to ask for compromises. Think of your preferences as the ideal way of responding to your needs. Making slight compromises will still ensure your needs are fulfilled; however, it may not be in the ideal form you expect. For example, your partner may agree to spend quality time with the TV switched off on weeknights except when a sports game is playing or on Friday nights when they prefer to go out with friends.

Step 3: Write Down Your Deal-Breakers

After you have written your preferences, it is time to write down your deal-breakers. These are nonnegotiable boundaries that cannot be debated. The message to your partner is simple: *Either you adhere to this boundary or all bets are off*.

Every human being has deal-breakers, things that we cannot overlook or tolerate in our relationships. For some, this could be cheating and, for others, domestic violence. Nevertheless, these are the lines that cannot be crossed, otherwise the relationship will be over.

To identify your deal-breakers, take a few days or weeks to think back to devastating experiences that have threatened your physical, mental, or emotional health in past romantic relationships. These could have also been experiences that occurred between you and your parents. Consider what violations took place that caused significant pain and suffering. These violations will form part of your nonnegotiable boundaries.

Here are a few examples of deal-breakers to get you thinking:

- cheating
- physical assault
- sexual assault
- substance abuse
- gambling
- harming animals and children
- stealing material possessions

When you have figured out what type of boundaries you need and determined your preferences and deal-breakers, the final step is to put it all together in a well-crafted message and communicate your boundaries to your partner.

Communicating Boundaries With the DESO Technique

It takes a lot of time, reflection, and planning to figure out what boundaries to establish to address the power imbalance and other issues you may be experiencing in your relationship. After going through all of that effort, you owe it to yourself to communicate your boundaries with conviction and confidence.

Understandably, you may be afraid of what your partner will say or how they might react after presenting your boundaries. This is a common fear for people who are not yet comfortable expressing their needs. To help you prepare for this type of conversation, you can practice what is called the Describe, Express, Specify, Outcome (DESO) technique (Related Perspectives, 2020).

The DESO technique is a communication tool that helps you organize your thoughts and emotions so that you can convey messages clearly and coherently. This technique is great to use when you are preparing to have tough conversations that require openness and honesty. The four steps outlined in the technique can also help you present information directly and assertively so that you can get your messages across without being thrown off by your partner.

Outlined below are the four steps to practice the DESO technique and examples to show you how (Related Perspectives, 2020).

Step 1: Describe

Describe the situation that calls for a boundary. This could be a recent behavior you didn't like or a recurring pattern you are noticing in your relationship. When describing the situation, be as objective as possible. Do not make any accusations about what is happening; instead, point out what you have seen and experienced in real life.

Here are a few examples:

- "I have noticed that you give me the silent treatment whenever you don't get your way."

- "Yesterday, at the dinner table, you spoke unkindly toward me in front of the kids."
- "When I shared the good news with you earlier today, you shrugged it off and didn't congratulate me."

Step 2: Express

Express how the once-off or recurring pattern of behavior makes you feel. Use "I" statements to show ownership of your emotions and avoid passing blame. It is up to you to decide how detailed you want to be when sharing your emotional experience. However, realize that since narcissists lack empathy, you may need to make an example they can relate to for them to understand the impact of their behaviors.

Here are a few examples:

- "I feel diminished when you ignore me as though what I am saying doesn't matter to you."
- "I feel embarrassed when you talk down on me in front of the kids. Imagine if a colleague at work put you down in a board room meeting."
- "I feel unappreciated when you don't praise me for my achievements. How would you feel if I stopped encouraging you for the hard work you do in taking care of our family?"

Step 3: Specify

Once you have described the situation that calls for a boundary and expressed how it makes you feel, the third step is to specify what you would like to see happening. This is where your preference, or negotiable boundary, comes in. Be clear on the alternative behavior you would like to see your partner performing. Make your request specific so that they know what to do. Bear in mind that your partner may seek a compromise if they are not completely comfortable fulfilling your request.

Here are a few examples:

- "I would like for you to express that you need space and some time to think instead of going silent."
- "I would like for you to speak respectfully toward me in front of the kids so they can show the same respect toward me too."
- "The next time I achieve a goal, I would like for you to say, "Well done" and acknowledge my hard work."

Step 4: Outcome

The fourth step is to explain the outcomes of not honoring your boundaries. In other words, present the consequences for continued bad behaviors. Once again, your consequences should be plain and simple so that your partner understands the implications of their behaviors. Note that your consequences are nonnegotiable and must be carried out consistently every time the boundary is violated.

Here are a few examples:

- "If you continue to give me the silent treatment whenever you don't get your way, then I will stop being quick to respond to your needs."
- "If you continue to speak unkindly toward me in front of our kids, then I will have no choice but to point out your bad behavior in front of them."
- "If you continue to shrug off my accomplishments, I won't show any interest in your accomplishments either."

Practicing these four simple steps will help you communicate your boundaries effectively and begin to express your needs. Please note that using the DESO technique doesn't guarantee that your partner will adhere to your boundaries. However, it does allow you to set limits and start enforcing consequences for boundary violations. In other words, you get to correct your partner whenever they act in ways that go against your wishes.

How to Create and Enforce Consequences for Boundary Violations

When you have gotten over the hurdle of communicating your boundaries, it is crucial to follow through by creating and enforcing the most suitable consequences. Boundaries without consequences are ineffective because they don't hold others accountable for their behaviors, and as a result, there is less motivation for them to honor your limits.

One reason why you may be reluctant to create and enforce consequences is that you are afraid of coming across as punitive. While at face value, consequences may seem like a form of retaliation for not having your needs met, they are positive accountability measures you create to reduce undesirable behaviors. Think of consequences as a way of teaching your partner the difference between acceptable and unacceptable behavior and helping them learn how to treat you better.

Due to narcissistic people's inability to put themselves in others' shoes, they need to be shown repeatedly how some of their behaviors negatively impact others. Unlike most people, they tend to not feel bad or guilty for crossing your boundaries. Consequences can alert your narcissistic partner whenever they have crossed the line and remind them of what good behavior looks like.

Another benefit of creating and enforcing consequences is that you can start to reclaim power in your relationship. This is extremely important if you intend to remain in this type of romantic relationship. Over the years, due to psychological manipulation, a power imbalance has occurred in your relationship that has threatened your sense of safety and ability to have your needs met. Consequences show your partner that you are serious about preventing certain harmful behaviors from continuing. Furthermore, they limit the number of chances you give to your partner to change and work with you to rebuild your union.

There are a few things to consider when creating and enforcing consequences. The first is whether it is the first time your partner is violating your boundary or if they have a recurring pattern of violating your boundary. The consequences imposed in both instances will be different. Your consequence for a first-time violation should be more lenient than a consequence for a repeat violation. This is because you must make a positive assumption that your partner wasn't aware of the impact of their actions.

For example, if it is the first time that your partner crosses a boundary by speaking badly about your close family, you can simply restate your boundary and the consequence, then ask them not to do it again. Your response may sound like:

"I have told you before that I don't want you to bad mouth my close family. I feel guilty because of being caught in the middle of people whom I love. Please refrain from bringing up anything negative about my family to me. If you continue, I will have to walk away from the conversation."

Let's assume they don't take your warning seriously and violate the boundary once again, what happens now? This is when you will need to follow through by enforcing the consequence. Instead of repeating the boundary and consequence, take action. Do exactly what you had said you were going to do and walk away, without explaining.

Something else worth considering is the different types of consequences you set for negotiable (preferences) and nonnegotiable (deal-breakers) boundaries. For instance, with negotiable boundaries, your consequences are supposed to encourage desirable behaviors by creating unpleasant experiences whenever your partner behaves poorly. This is done as many times as required to modify your partner's behaviors. The consequences set for nonnegotiable boundaries are supposed to enforce final action that ends the relationship or places permanent restrictions on what your partner can and cannot do.

For example, if one of your deal-breakers is cheating, the consequence could be to either leave the romantic relationship, move out of the home where you both reside, or enforce a semi-permanent separation. As you can tell, these consequences convey the seriousness of the offense and make it clear what you cannot tolerate.

Lastly, expect your partner to resist or throw a fit whenever you enforce consequences. Their anger comes from the fact that you are challenging and confronting their harmful behaviors. Don't allow this to intimidate you (as this is probably the motive behind your partner's explosive emotions). Practice masking your vulnerability and walk away with the conversation when it feels unsafe (refer to Chapter 6).

Chapter 9

Rewrite Your Life Script

You are the author of your own life story. You have the leading role and get to determine how you interact with your supporting cast and other characters.

— SUSAN C. YOUNG

The Importance of Rewriting Your Life Script

*E*very human being has a story they tell themselves about their lives. *This story is known as a life script.*

Think for a moment about the normal progression of a film or fictional book. The story of the main character is told through a sequence of events and details a period in their life where conflict and growth take place. The story told about your life takes on a similar structure. How you remember your childhood, adolescence, and adult years is summarized in a sequence of events or a timeline and includes periods of conflict and growth.

Depending on your perspective about your life and where you are on your healing journey, how you tell the story will be different. For example, telling the story about your childhood while still grappling with abandonment wounds will take a different tone than when you tell the same story during the process of healing these hurts. The same goes for your relationship with your partner. How you described your relationship during the honeymoon stage is not the same as how you describe the current state of your relationship.

Due to the natural shifts in your perspective, especially after you have gained a better understanding of your life, it is important to rethink and retell your life script. You are not the person you were five years ago, a year ago, or before reading this book. Your mind is constantly expanding and adapting to the knowledge you absorb about who you are and what you are capable of, such as how you perceive your life and relationships, must also be adjusted.

One of the things that can hold you back when seeking to recover and break free from narcissistic abuse is holding on to a negative life script. Your negative life script could be informed by unresolved childhood issues, past break-ups you haven't yet healed from, or carrying a sense of shame about surviving abuse. You might undeservedly take the blame for people and situations that caused you a lot of pain, and as a result, you take on a dark perspective about your life.

A negative life script can delay your recovery because it triggers old wounds. Instead of perceiving difficulties from the past as one part of your story, you may erroneously make them the center of your story and struggle to move on. Moreover, you may unconsciously repeat and reinforce harmful coping mechanisms and behavioral patterns in current relationships, which keeps you in a toxic loop and prevents you from rebuilding your life.

Retell Your Story in Your Own Words

Rewriting your life script involves reflecting on what you believe about yourself and various aspects of your life. Bear in mind that as a child, your immediate family and community condition you to believe certain ideas about yourself. Since you were still too young to question those beliefs, you accepted them as the truth. The disadvantage, however, is that if those beliefs were negative, you may have grown up with a negative life script.

As an adult, you get to journey as far back into the past as you would like and question beliefs that you were taught explicitly or implicitly. Explicit beliefs were ideas you heard being repeated to you, whereas implicit beliefs were ideas you learned through modeled behaviors. For example, if a parent often said, "Your opinions don't matter," you may have grown up believing they were correct—your opinions didn't matter. However, if they got distracted or looked away whenever you were speaking to them, the same message—"Your opinions don't matter"—was passed to you.

The purpose of rewriting your life script is to search for these negative explicit and implicit beliefs in your life story and change your perspective about what happened. For example, you can reflect on your parent looking away whenever you were speaking to them and consider what else might have been happening. There must be more to the story that you can see now that you are much older than what you saw as a child. You may find that since you know that your parent was living with depression, they were unable to provide consistent nurturing. Their behavior was a symptom of them being emotionally overwhelmed and feeling the need to withdraw rather than it being a sign of not valuing your opinions.

Or perhaps you grew up believing that true love doesn't exist. This could have been an implicit belief adopted as a result of hot-and-cold parenting. However, when looking back at how affection was shown, you may be able to see that you had an anxious attachment to your parents caused by inconsistencies in how and when they responded to your needs. Armed with this new information, you can now rewrite that portion of your life script and tell yourself that true love does exist; however, it exists between two conscious and healed individuals who are secure within themselves.

As you can see, retelling your story is a process that takes a lot of time. It requires you to adjust your outlook on your life, one past event, belief, and experience at a time. To start, you can focus on adjusting the core problematic beliefs you hold about your life, then as time goes by, work on correcting the smaller beliefs that distort your outlook.

Out With the Old Beliefs and in With the New

During the process of rewriting your life script, you will need to identify limiting or negative self-beliefs and replace them with empowering ones. Limiting self-beliefs create mental barriers that are difficult to overcome. *They tell you who you cannot be and what you cannot achieve.*

When your mind is full of limiting self-beliefs, you tend to focus on your weaknesses. These become amplified to the extent of convincing yourself that you don't have many strengths. Of course, this isn't true since every human being has just as many strengths as they have weaknesses.

Over time, self-limiting beliefs change how you view yourself. You may start to develop insecurities that make it difficult to relate in healthy ways with yourself and others. For example, believing that you are unattractive can make you critical about your appearance and self-conscious when entering a romantic relationship. Furthermore, feeling self-conscious could lead to problems with intimacy or seeking constant validation from your partner.

Identifying and replacing self-limiting beliefs won't just improve the quality of your romantic relationships; it can also improve the connection you have with yourself. What is more important than how others feel about you is how you feel about yourself. When you are capable of respecting who you are and advocating for your needs, certain poor behaviors toward you become unacceptable. Thinking highly of yourself can also attract people who are not intimidated by your strength and confidence, who instead encourage you to achieve greater heights!

If you are willing to start identifying and replacing self-limiting beliefs, you can use the following four strategies.

Acknowledge

Before you can replace a self-limiting belief, you must recognize it. As mentioned above, self-limiting beliefs tell you who you cannot be and what you cannot achieve. They can sound like a critical parent, school teacher, or supervisor who is never pleased with you. Examples of self-limiting beliefs are

- I am not good enough.
- I will never amount to anything.
- I can't survive on my own.
- I am difficult to love.
- Nobody will ever accept me for who I am.

Can you think of any other self-limiting beliefs that come to mind? Write them down on a piece of paper. These are going to be the beliefs that you confront and seek to address.

Validate

When self-limiting beliefs come to your mind, it is natural to try and push them away. This happens because some self-limiting beliefs can trigger and remind you of things you don't want to look at. However, to process and heal self-limiting beliefs, you must acknowledge and validate their existence.

Validation refers to accepting the reality of something, even if you don't agree with it. When you validate self-limiting beliefs, you accept the negative perceptions you hold about yourself and try to understand where they come from and what forced you to adopt those ideas. For instance, it is common to find self-limiting beliefs rooted in trauma, bullying, failure, and rejection. Most times, thinking poorly about yourself is a coping mechanism to prevent further pain.

Take out your list of self-limiting beliefs and go through each one. Read the belief out loud and then close your eyes and retrace where it originates. Go back in time and replay memories. Stop and take breathing breaks whenever you become emotional. Intuitively send messages to your younger self, telling them that they will be okay and life will get easier. You can send any other message that your younger self might appreciate.

Replace

Validating self-limiting beliefs allows you to accept the reality of how you currently view yourself. However, since they create a distorted idea of who you are, it is crucial to challenge and replace them. Challenging self-limiting beliefs requires you to pose open-ended questions and try to answer them as honestly as possible. How you answer these questions will prove whether the beliefs are true or false.

For example, if you believe that you are difficult to love, you might ask yourself, *Is this belief based on facts or emotions?* If it were based on facts, you would need sufficient evidence (personal encounters with more than one person, in more than one type of relationship) to prove it to be accurate. If it were based on emotions, then you can conclude that it is an opinion and, therefore, cannot be treated as the truth.

Other open-ended questions you can ask include

- What are the pros and cons of this belief?
- What other information haven't I considered?
- Would the next person share the same belief about me?
- Was this belief inherited from someone?
- Does this belief consider my growth?

After challenging self-limiting beliefs, you can rule them out to be true or false and replace them with fair and balanced ideas that acknowledge both your strengths and weaknesses. Imagine that you are a judge in court and have to present a ruling about your self-limiting beliefs. Take into consideration the evidence gathered about your beliefs and come up with fair and balanced beliefs to replace them.

For example, after discovering that your belief that "I am difficult to love" is inaccurate, you might come up with the following replacement: *Yes, I have a fiery personality that causes clashes between me and others, but those who love and accept me can attest to how much of a kind and compassionate person I am.*

Set Positive Intentions for Today

Rewriting your life script isn't solely about looking into the past and adjusting your understanding of what happened, but it is also about embracing the present moment and setting positive intentions for the life you desire.

As someone who is recovering from narcissistic abuse, it can be difficult for you to believe that being content with your life is possible. Perhaps, over the years, your primary concern has been on maintaining your relationship, which has caused you to disconnect from who you are and what makes you happy.

Now that you are beginning to prioritize yourself again, it is crucial to think big when it comes to recreating the life of your dreams.

Surviving narcissistic abuse is a victory that you will continue to celebrate for the rest of your life. Since you have managed to unhook yourself from your narcissistic partner's grip, it is time to reclaim lost aspects of your life by reshaping your future, one positive daily intention at a time.

Positive intentions are daily reminders of who you are and what you need at the moment. Unlike goals that focus on planning for the future, positive intentions encourage you to live as though you have already accomplished your goals. The aim is to align yourself with your desired physical, mental, and emotional state by creating aspirations for every day. Gradually, your positive intentions will enable you to adopt new habits and transform the way you live.

Positive intentions look and feel differently for everyone because no two individuals' needs are identical. Therefore, when setting positive intentions tune in to how you feel upon waking up and what type of day you would like to have. If something is weighing on your mind, perhaps you can create an intention to help you cope with the situation. Or if you are preparing to do something brave, set an intention to inspire courage and confidence.

Setting positive intentions is about visualizing how you would like to feel at the end of the day or after a particular task or event. Furthermore, it is about imagining the best possible outcomes when engaging with others, trying out new experiences, or venturing outside of your comfort zone. Your positive intentions are also based on the things that matter the most to you, such as your values, beliefs, morals, and boundaries.

As you begin to work on creating positive intentions for today, consider the following suggestions as inspiration:

- I intend to be patient with myself and others.
- I intend to approach new situations with curiosity.
- I intend to do my best with the tools I have and let go of what I cannot control.
- I intend to allow others to be themselves and reveal who they are.
- I intend to live in the moment and focus on what is happening now.
- I intend to align my actions with my highest desires.
- I intend to be my authentic self even when it is not popular.
- I intend to share my thoughts and feelings even when I am afraid.
- I intend to see each experience as a learning opportunity.
- I intend to think compassionate thoughts that bring out the best in me.

Chapter 10

How to Repel Narcissists in the Dating World

When we meet and fall into the gravitational pull of a narcissist, we are entering a significant life lesson that involves learning how to create boundaries, self-respect, and resilience.

–MATEO SOL

How to Identify Narcissists in Online Dating

Reclaiming your power is about enforcing boundaries, updating your life script, replacing self-limiting beliefs, and setting positive intentions about the experiences and life you desire. However, concerning healing from narcissistic abuse, reclaiming your power is about making sure you don't date or marry another narcissist!

In high school, you were never taught how to date with caution. All you learned was that dating could lead to sex and regrettable diseases. At home, your parents may have overlooked this topic, too, choosing not to bring up dating at all or giving you free rein to explore the dating scene and learn for yourself.

As a result, when you started dating, you had limited knowledge and experience about what you were getting into. You didn't know what to look for in a partner and common signs that you were talking to someone with narcissistic tendencies. Now that you are older and wiser—and have enough experience dating narcissists to know that is not what you want moving forward—you can start to date differently.

Online dating has become the easiest way to connect with local and international singles. Through sophisticated dating apps that can match you with people who fall under your search criteria (e.g. tall, brown eyes, without kids), you can meet new people by a simple swipe rather than physically going to local social spots.

The online dating world is populated by different types of people. Some good-intentioned people are upfront about who they are attracted to and what type of relationship dynamic they want. However, among them are some predators who create profiles to find their next unsuspecting victims and dupe them into believing they have good intentions. Narcissists fall under the group of predators who use online dating for self-gain.

Unfortunately, dating apps do not indicate which profiles are sincere and which ones are fake. It is your job to discern whether or not to continue chatting with someone based on the information they have provided. Narcissists will not make it obvious that they have ulterior motives; however, since many of those who create online dating profiles are overt narcissists, there are a few ways to identify them, such as

- **They look too good to be true**: Someone who is extremely focused on their image and beauty could be disguising character flaws. Beauty is also used as a trick to create an illusion of grandiosity, being high status, and being the ideal partner. People with genuine motives don't

mind being seen for who they are and showing normal
aspects of their lives.

- **They don't have friends**: Someone who claims to not
  trust people may not be trustworthy. A narcissist is known
  to be a loner or has superficial relationships with
  acquaintances and colleagues. They often have strained
  relationships with family and make their romantic
  relationship the center of their life.

- **They prefer not to have labels**: Someone who doesn't
  want labels is either a commitment-phobe or a narcissist
  who doesn't want to be bound by rules. Labels create
  expectations and routines, which they are not willing to
  follow. They might try to convince you that labels are
  outdated and love should not be defined.

- **They enjoy talking about themselves**: Someone who
  gets excited when asked about themselves but looks bored
  or disinterested when listening to you share about yourself
  may be self-centered and lack empathy. In committed
  relationships, they tend to be unsupportive and throw
  tantrums when the focus is not on them.

- **They rush intimacy**: Someone who brings up the topic of
  intimacy early on or makes sexual comments may be more
  interested in what you can offer them than getting to know
  you. Since a narcissist seeks to win trust as soon as possible,
  they tend to rush intimacy and get you emotionally
  invested in the relationship.

Please note you cannot always tell from reading information on a
profile whether someone has narcissistic tendencies or not,
particularly when they are a covert or malignant narcissist. They may
be so good at coming across as sincere that they don't sound any

alarms. In this case, you may need to go on a few dates and get to know them better to understand who they truly are.

First Date Signs That You Are With a Narcissist

It is possible to miss or not see any signs of narcissism when initially connecting with someone. However, on the first date, you get to interact with them in person and pick up on signals you were unable to detect over the phone. There are obvious signs of narcissism:

- not asking questions to get to know you
- showing no emotion when sharing a personal experience
- laughing at stories about your misfortune
- badmouthing their exes, including friends and family they no longer speak to
- name-dropping and signaling their wealth or success
- speaking about themselves in the third person
- being opinionated about what they like and dislike in other people
- being rude or impatient with waiters and waitresses
- feeling entitled to hold your hand or show other forms of intimacy
- being particular about where they sit, how they prefer their meal, and what traditions should be practiced at the table

There are other nonobvious signs that you are sitting across from a narcissistic individual. These signs are often sensed on an intuitive level, and there may not be any evidence to support your inclinations. Nevertheless, since the relationship is still fresh, it is safer to go with your gut instinct than to believe the words or actions of someone you barely know.

Some of the nonobvious signs to look out for include

- **They don't seem present**: Your date may be saying all of the right things and being a perfect gentleman, but you don't feel an openness about them. Instead, they may seem like they are overthinking or following steps learned from a handbook.

- **They don't show genuine interest**: Your date may nod, maintain eye contact, and ask questions, but there is a haunting emptiness that you sense when you look into their eyes. They appear detached whenever you start sharing personal information and come alive again when the conversation becomes superficial.

- **You feel like you are being studied**: The way that your date scans your face and body or seems deep in thought whenever you are sharing a story makes you feel vulnerable. It is like they are waiting to catch you out or trying to look deep into your soul.

- **They did at least one thing that was shocking and out of character**: It is part of a narcissist's game to test your boundaries early on. Thus, your date may have done something outrageous or out of character and then immediately brushed it off or waited for you to say something.

- **They make jokes that feel like put-downs**: After sharing something about your life, your date may tell a joke to mock or make light of your experience. This may be followed by loud bolts of laughter and animated gestures to make you join in and laugh at yourself. However, the joke is often embarrassing or insensitive and makes you look bad.

How to Repel Narcissism in the Dating World

After breaking free from narcissistic abuse, you may vow to never get into a relationship with another toxic individual. Nevertheless, this may not be enough to prevent predators like narcissists from trying their luck with you in the future.

It goes back to what we had spoken about earlier in the book about who narcissists are attracted to. Initially, narcissists are not picky about whom they will approach and will decide later on if their love interests are worth pursuing based on the vulnerabilities they reveal. Repelling narcissism is, therefore, not about making rigid dating rules that make it difficult for people to get to know you but, rather, working on building your self-worth and displaying behaviors that make you come across as a difficult person to manipulate.

Here are a few empowering behaviors you can start practicing that drive narcissists crazy—and not in a good way!

Don't Wait for a Compliment—Boost Your Own Confidence

Cultivate a positive self-image that isn't based on being in a romantic relationship. Spend time getting to know yourself outside of your relationship roles (e.g., daughter, friend, partner, employee) and discover new strengths, passions, desires, and talents about yourself. It is also important to be aware of your character flaws and where they stem from. Go through the process of accepting, validating, and replacing self-limiting beliefs so that you can start becoming your cheerleader. This will ensure that when you meet someone, you are not expecting them to boost your confidence with compliments or validation. The message you will be sending across is clear: What they think about you matters but not as much as how much you value and cherish yourself!

Turn Off the "Empathy Switch" When There Is No Reciprocation

Don't be quick to do favors or offer emotional support to someone you have just met, especially when you haven't given your relationship a label or made any real commitments to each other. Learn the difference between validating and empathizing with someone. Validation is about accepting their reality for what it is, while empathy requires you to step into their shoes and imagine what they may be feeling.

Moreover, be mindful not to do any emotional labor without reciprocation. For example, do not call your partner to check how their day went if they are unable to do the same with you. The amount of care and attention you give to your partner should be similar to what they offer you. If that is not the case, cut back on how much you invest into the relationship. Find other healthy relationships to express your love and devotion, such as relationships with close friends and family or your pets.

Keep Yourself Busy and Fill Your Calendar With Meaningful Activities

During the early stages of a relationship, do not deviate from your routines and commitments. Continue to prioritize your health, work, friendships, and other goals you may have. The amount of time allocated to spending time with your partner should be something you discuss together. Being with each other should not interfere with your lifestyle or close relationships with friends and family. Instead, it should complement your lifestyle and flow with everything you have going on.

Freeing up more time to spend with your partner should come with conditions, such as having a serious conversation about where your relationship is heading, being open about expectations that both of you may have, and reasonable compromises that both of you can make to allow for more time together. Essentially, the need for spending more time together should be something you both share and are willing to make sacrifices for.

Don't Fight for the Relationship at the Beginning

At the beginning of the relationship, you are gathering information about your partner so that you can learn about who they are. This is usually when you identify positive qualities, bad habits, and red flags that you cannot ignore. Bad habits can be ironed out in the future, but red flags will only get worse with time. Therefore, it is recommended to hold back on making any commitments too soon after meeting someone to allow yourself enough time to see their true colors. If you sense or notice a red flag (refer to Chapter 1), then it is safe to say that you have found a good reason to discontinue pursuing a romantic relationship with the individual (Who knows? You might end up being good friends).

Wouldn't it be great if you could build an immunity to narcissism? Unfortunately, there isn't a vaccine that can assist you with that yet! In the meantime, remember that narcissists only have as much power as you are willing to give them. Reclaim your power in the relationship, and they won't have a reason to stay!

Conclusion

Narcissistic love is riding on the rollercoaster of disaster filled with a heart full of tears.

– SHEREE GRIFFIN

You should never blame yourself for falling in love with a narcissist. This undercover predator has spent years studying human behavior and crafting their impenetrable mask. They are masters at creating illusions and getting you to buy into the fantasy they have created where they are the ideal lover—*who can both build you up and tear you down.*

The kind of love you receive during the early stages of being with a narcissistic partner cannot be compared to anything that you have ever felt for someone before. The best way to describe it is the feeling of coming home to yourself. Your partner brings out a side of you that you didn't know existed and promises to give you the affection you wished for as a child.

In hindsight, you come to learn that what you felt for your partner wasn't true love but infatuation. If it was true love, you wouldn't have lost sight of who you are, abandoned other meaningful experiences in your life, or felt heartache every time you thought about your partner leaving.

Narcissistic abuse is real even though it doesn't always leave physical scars.

Your partner, who may or may not be diagnosed with NPD, takes you on an unforgettable roller coaster ride, going from extreme highs to extreme lows. The only way to get off this ride is to recognize that you are in an abusive relationship where the only thing your partner wants is control.

The purpose of this book was to expose narcissism for what it truly is—another form of emotional abuse—and provide you with the tools and strategies to break free from narcissistic abuse. This was achieved by introducing you to the 3 "Rs" which are Recognize, Respond, and Reclaim.

- **Recognize**: The first step to unhooking yourself from your partner's grip is to recognize that you are in an abusive relationship where psychological manipulation tactics are used to pull you down and distort your sense of reality.
- **Respond**: The second step is to rebuild your psychological defense by learning how to communicate and interact with your partner in a manner that won't allow them to get away with hurting you. This is also the perfect time to leave a narcissistic abusive relationship; however, remember to do so with caution.
- **Reclaim**: The third step is to reclaim your power by addressing vulnerabilities that make you an easy target to your narcissists. This may include creating and enforcing boundaries, rewriting your life script, and challenging self-limiting beliefs.

Part of recovering from narcissistic abuse is accepting the fact that you cannot change your partner, you can only change how you engage with them. NPD is a serious disorder that has lifelong effects. If you choose to stay with a partner who suffers from this condition, building a strong sense of self and healing from your own past traumas is the best way to restore the power balance.

Continue to make yourself a priority and practice the 3 Rs (Recognize, Respond, and Reclaim) to heal from narcissistic abuse and build the kind of romantic relationship you desire.

Congratulations on finishing the book and learning about narcissism. If you have found the information valuable, consider purchasing a copy for a cousin, friend, or colleague! If you have found it helpful to learn more about narcissistic abuse and how to break the abuse cycle, please leave a review on Amazon!

Glossary

Boundaries: Personal limits that you set with others to protect you from exploitative behaviors.

Childhood neglect: The continuous failure to notice or respond to a child's needs.

Codependency: The obsessive need to gain approval from others, usually at one's own expense.

Consequences: The unpleasant outcomes of violating boundaries.

Deal-breakers: Nonnegotiable boundaries that warrant harsh consequences.

DESO technique: A communication tool used to communicate boundaries clearly and coherently.

Gut instinct: The sixth sense or intuitive feeling you get when you know something to be true but have no evidence to show.

Narcissism: An extreme form of self-centeredness that causes a lack of empathy for others.

Narcissistic abuse: A type of emotional abuse committed by people who display signs of narcissism.

Narcissistic abuse cycle: The three-step process narcissists take their victims through to lower their psychological defenses and inflict harm.

Narcissistic abuse support groups: Virtual or in-person meetings where survivors of narcissistic abuse meet and share experiences to encourage each other.

Narcissistic personality disorder: A mental health disorder recognized in the DSM-5 that is characterized by an unreasonably high self-importance.

Narcissistic supply: People who are targeted and become victims of narcissists.

Preferences: Negotiable boundaries that describe ideal ways you would like others to respond to your needs.

Psychological manipulation: Controlling how someone thinks or feels through coercion or persuasive tactics.

Survivor: An individual who has broken free from the narcissistic abuse cycle.

Victim: An individual who is still within the narcissistic abuse cycle.

About the Author

Cameron J. Clark, MSW, MFCC, is a dedicated life coach, passionate about empowering women who have experienced abusive relationships or struggle with low self-esteem and self-love. Drawing from her journey of overcoming an unhappy and abusive past, Cameron has transformed her life and is now happily thriving in a loving relationship.

With her compassionate and empathetic approach, she is committed to helping others find their inner strength, rebuild their confidence, and create healthy, fulfilling relationships. Cameron's unique coaching style combines practical strategies with emotional support, enabling her clients to break free from the chains of their past and embrace a future full of hope and joy.

When she's not guiding and inspiring women to reclaim their lives, Cameron enjoys spending quality time with her loved ones and her beloved dog, Luca. An avid reader, she finds solace and inspiration in the pages of a good book. Cameron also cherishes her wine nights with friends, celebrating the beautiful bonds of sisterhood and the journey they share toward healing and self-discovery.

References

Ambardar, S. (2021). Narcissistic personality disorder: Practice essentials, background, pathophysiology and etiology. *EMedicine*. https://emedicine.medscape.com/article/1519417-overview?form=fpf

Arabi, S. (2018, July 24). *5 signs of narcissists in dating*. Psych Central. https://psychcentral.com/blog/recovering-narcissist/2018/07/5-dating-red-flags-of-narcissists-we-mistake-for-intimacy#1

Arabi, S. (2019, August 31). *5 powerful ways to turn off narcissists, sociopaths, and psychopaths - how to protect yourself in dating*. Psych Central. https://psychcentral.com/blog/recovering-narcissist/2019/08/5-powerful-ways-to-turn-off-narcissists-sociopaths-and-psychopaths-how-to-protect-yourself-in-dating#1

Baker, J. (2021, March 3). *Why your boundaries are not welcome in an abusive relationship*. A Space to Reflect. https://aspacetoreflect.com/2021/03/03/why-your-boundaries-are-not-welcome-in-an-abusive-relationship/

Being, G. (2023, July 9). *Narcissistic abuse therapy*. Grace Being. https://grace-being.com/love-relationships/narcissistic-abuse-therapy/#google_vignette

Brown, B. (2022, June 14). 140+ quotes about narcissists to help you better understand and recognize the behavior. *Woman's Day*. https://www.womansday.com/life/a40059190/narcissist-quotes/

Carter, N. (2021, May 28). *A guide to developing intuition: 12 ways to tap into your inner knowing*. Skillshare Blog. https://www.skillshare.com/en/blog/a-guide-to-developing-intuition-12-ways-to-tap-into-your-inner-knowing/

Childs Heyl, J. (2022, June 23). *How to find a narcissistic abuse support group*. Verywell Mind. https://www.verywellmind.com/how-to-find-a-narcissistic-abuse-support-group-5271477#toc-seeking-support

Cleveland Clinic. (2014). *Narcissistic personality disorder*. https://my.clevelandclinic.org/health/diseases/9742-narcissistic-personality-disorder

Creating a safety plan. (2015). In *British Columbia*. https://www2.gov.bc.ca/assets/gov/law-crime-and-justice/criminal-justice/victims-of-crime/vs-info-for-professionals/training/creating-safety-plan.pdf

Davenport, B. (2023, January 16). *Pay attention to your gut with these 27 signs you're meant to be with someone*. Live Bold and Bloom. https://liveboldandbloom.com/01/relationships/gut-feeling-signs-someone

Degges-White, S. (2022, October 11). *Can a narcissist love?*
Choosing Therapy.
https://www.choosingtherapy.com/can-a-narcissist-love/#

Delony, J. (2023, August 24). *10 signs you're in a toxic relationship.*
Ramsey Solutions.
https://www.ramseysolutions.com/relationships/toxic-
relationship-signs

Denise. (2023, June 16). *Rewriting your life script.* Mind Reset.
https://www.mindreset.co.uk/2023/06/16/rewriting-
your-life-script/

Dodgson, L. (2023, April 14). *The 5 types of people narcissists are
attracted to, according to relationship experts.* Insider.
https://www.insider.com/the-types-of-people-narcissists-
are-attracted-to-2018-8#its-all-about-control-6

Dr. Lurve. (2020, January 13). *5 signs your Tinder date is probably a
narcissist.* Amodrn. https://amodrn.com/five-signs-your-
tinder-date-is-probably-a-narcissist/

Durvasula, R. (n.d.). *Ramani Durvasula quote.* Goodreads.
https://www.goodreads.com/author/show/5813517.Ram
ani_Durvasula

Fox, E. (2023, October 6). *Best narcissist quotes that help you
understand them better.* Style Craze.
https://www.stylecraze.com/articles/narcissist-quotes/

Franzen, J. (n.d.). *Jonathan Franzen quote.* Goodreads.
https://www.goodreads.com/author/show/2578.Jonatha
n_Franzen

Gillette, H. (2022, October 5). *What is emotional manipulation?*
Psych Central. https://psychcentral.com/health/signs-of-
psychological-and-emotional-manipulation#tips

Gordon, S. (2020, December 27). *How to put together a safety plan when you're being abused*. Verywell Mind. https://www.verywellmind.com/making-a-safety-plan-to-escape-abusive-relationship-5069959

Greenberg, E. (2020, July 17). *Why narcissists twist the truth*. Psychology Today. https://www.psychologytoday.com/za/blog/understanding-narcissism/202007/why-narcissists-twist-the-truth

Griffin, S. (2023, October 6). *Best narcissist quotes that help you understand them better*. Style Craze. https://www.stylecraze.com/articles/narcissist-quotes/#google_vignette

Hailey, L. (n.d.). *How to set boundaries: 5 Ways to draw the line politely*. Science of People. https://www.scienceofpeople.com/how-to-set-boundaries/

Holland, M. (2022, May 3). *17 manipulation tactics abusers use*. Choosing Therapy. https://www.choosingtherapy.com/manipulation-tactics/

How to plan for your safety if you are in an abusive relationship. (2011, July 4). Canada. https://www.canada.ca/en/public-health/services/health-promotion/stop-family-violence/plan-your-safety.html

Ishler, J. (2023, February 8). *30+ journal prompts to help you improve your relationships*. The Everygirl. https://theeverygirl.com/relationships-journal-prompts/

Jones, D. M. (n.d.). *Codependency quotes (146 quotes)*. Goodreads. https://www.goodreads.com/quotes/tag/codependency

Kholghi, B. (2021, December 15). *11 best ways to emotionally detach from a narcissist 2022*. Coaching Online.

https://www.coaching-online.org/how-to-emotionally-detach-from-a-narcissist/

Lancer, D. (2019, May 5). *Why narcissists act the way they do*. Psych Central. https://psychcentral.com/lib/why-narcissists-act-the-way-they-do#1

Malone, T. (2022, June 14). 140+ quotes about narcissists to help you better understand and recognize the behavior. *Woman's Day*. https://www.womansday.com/life/a40059190/narcissist-quotes/

McDowall, S. (2020, February 19). *Narcissism and the trauma of narcissistic abuse*. Farah Therapy Centre. https://www.farahtherapycentre.co.uk/blog/narcissism-and-the-trauma-of-narcissistic-abuse

Moore, M. (2013, September 8). *Narcissist and codependent compatibility in relationships*. Psych Central. https://psychcentral.com/disorders/the-dance-between-codependents-narcissists#codependent-vs-narcissist

Morgan, E. (2021, November 12). *When to trust your gut instinct (& when to ignore it)*. Refinery29. https://www.refinery29.com/en-us/2021/11/10751082/should-you-trust-your-gut-instinct

Neuharth, D. (2017, September 14). *How narcissists react to information about narcissism*. Psych Central. https://psychcentral.com/blog/psychology-self/2018/11/narcissists-information-narcissism#2

Powell, W. (2015, February 3). *10 ways to discourage narcissists from dating you*. Wendy J Powell. https://wendyjpowell.wordpress.com/2015/02/03/10-ways-to-discourage-narcissists-from-dating-you-2/

Regan, S. (2021, February 26). *Gut feelings: What they really are & how to know if you can trust them*. MindBodyGreen. https://www.mindbodygreen.com/articles/gut-feelings-what-they-really-are-when-to-trust-them

Related Perspectives. (2020, July 24). *Assertive communication: The DESO framework*. https://www.relatedperspectives.com/post/assertive-communication-the-deso-framework

Rewriting life scripts for personal growth. (n.d.). Eightify App. https://eightify.app/summary/personal-development-and-self-improvement/rewriting-life-scripts-for-personal-growth

Rice, A. (n.d.). *Anne Rice quote*. Goodreads. https://www.goodreads.com/author/show/7577.Anne_Rice

Saeed, K. (2020, January 15). *REAL self-care ideas for new survivors of narcissistic abuse*. Kim Saeed. https://kimsaeed.com/2020/01/14/real-self-care-ideas-for-new-survivors-of-narcissistic-abuse/

Sanford, K. (2019). *Partner Reading 3: My boundary was violated, now what?! (A guide for partners)*. Banyan Therapy. https://www.banyantherapy.com/wp-content/uploads/2019/02/Partner-Reading-3-My-Boundary-was-Just-Violated-%E2%80%93-Now-What.pdf

Saxena, S. (2021, November 18). *What is a narcissistic abuse cycle & how does it work?* Choosing Therapy. https://www.choosingtherapy.com/narcissistic-abuse-cycle/

Sissons, B. (2022, October 5). *Narcissistic abuse: Definition, signs, and recovery*. MedicalNewsToday.

https://www.medicalnewstoday.com/articles/narcissistic-abuse#the-signs

Smith, S. (2021, August 26). *Why you need to trust the gut feeling in relationships*. Marriage. https://www.marriage.com/advice/relationship/gut-instinct-in-relationships/

Sol, M. (2023, October 6). *Best narcissist quotes that help you understand them better*. Style Craze. https://www.stylecraze.com/articles/narcissist-quotes/#google_vignette

Synctuition. (2017, August 28). *Do you know when to trust your gut feeling?* Synctuition. https://synctuition.com/blog/know-when-to-trust-your-gut-feeling/

Telloian, C. (2021, September 15). *How many types of narcissism are there?* Psych Central. https://psychcentral.com/health/types-of-narcissism#5-types-of-narcissism

Torroni, A. (2022, June 14). 140+ quotes about narcissists to help you better understand and recognize the behavior. *Woman's Day*. https://www.womansday.com/life/a40059190/narcissist-quotes/

Touroni, E. (2020, October 2). *What are my needs? Identifying your emotional needs in a relationship*. The Chelsea Psychology Clinic. https://www.thechelseapsychologyclinic.com/sex-relationships/what-are-my-needs/

Up Journey. (2021, November 12). *How to communicate with a narcissist (30+ expert tips)*. https://upjourney.com/how-to-communicate-with-a-narcissist

Victoria. (2023, May 23). *15 tips for self-care after narcissistic abuse.* Unmasking the Narc. https://unmaskingthenarc.com/self-care-after-narcissistic-abuse/#STEP_6_Heal_Your_Inner_Wounds

Villamor, M. (2023, March 7). *How to create consequences for repeat boundary violations.* Terri Cole. https://www.terricole.com/boundary-violations/

Wolfe, J. S. (2023, May 3). *17 boundaries quotes.* Psych Central. https://psychcentral.com/health/quotes-healthy-boundaries#the-need-for-boundaries

Wright, S. A. (2022, February 28). *Love addiction: The stages of codependency.* Psych Central. https://psychcentral.com/addictions/stages-of-codependency-love-addiction#next-steps

Yandoli, K. (2023, October 25). *People revealed what it's like dating narcissists, and it's unfortunately eye-opening.* BuzzFeed. https://www.buzzfeed.com/kaylayandoli/dating-narcissist-stories

Young, S. C. (2016). *Susan C. Young quote.* Goodreads. https://www.goodreads.com/author/show/17169022.Susan_C_Young

Zucker, B. (2022, March 5). *3 ways to conquer negative beliefs about yourself.* Psychology Today. https://www.psychologytoday.com/za/blog/liberate-yourself/202203/3-ways-conquer-negative-beliefs-about-yourself

Printed in Dunstable, United Kingdom